JACK

An Incredible Life

JOLENA TAYLOR KING

REVIEW AND HERALD® PUBLISHING ASSOCIATION
HAGERSTOWN, MD 21740

The author assumes full responsibility for the accuracy of all facts and quotations as cited in this book.

This book was
Edited by Gerald Wheeler
Cover design by Bill Kirstein
Cover photo by Jim Marlowe
Typeset: 11/13 Garamond

PRINTED IN U.S.A.

02 01 00 99 98 5 4 3 2 1

R&H Cataloging Service
King, Jolena Taylor, 1940-
Jack—an incredible life.

1. Blanco, Jack John
I. Title. [B]

286.732092

ISBN 0-8280-1324-1

To order additional copies of *Jack—An Incredible Life,* by Jolena Taylor King, call 1-800-765-6955. For more information on Review and Herald products, visit us at www.rhpa.org

Dedication

This book is dedicated to
Kaylin, Taylor, Riley, and Chase
May you always love and trust your heavenly Father

CONTENTS

Chapter One

Rejected

"What do you *mean,* he doesn't work here any more? Do you know where he is? Do you have a forwarding address? This is very, *very* important!" Katie Kiesling fervently hoped her German accent did not reveal that she had spent only five short years in the United States. Nervous hands fidgeted with her empty purse.

"I'm sorry," the receptionist said, "Fredrick left no forwarding address." Her brusque return to the large stack of mail engulfing her desk inferred that the conversation was over, leaving Katie to figure out what to do next.

"I know!" she said to herself. "His landlady . . ."

She dashed down the busy sidewalk as fast as her tiny frame would go, her thoughts racing with her. The first day he had failed to call, she hadn't worried—not really. Not too much even the second day. "He could be out of town on business," she had reassured herself. But by the third day of not hearing from the man who had devoted himself so fully and passionately to her for the past several months, she was concerned enough to throw etiquette aside and call his apartment.

Fredrick was not there.

He must have had a real emergency come up to leave so suddenly without telling me. Or could there—she forced herself to think it—*could there have been an* accident? Chicago, even in 1928, was not the safest place in the world. Now, almost a week had passed and she had not received so much as one envelope with the familiar handwriting.

Mrs. McNamara was shaking a rug out the second-floor window when Katie arrived breathlessly. "Mrs. Mac," the younger woman called up to her timidly, "do you have any idea where Fredrick could be? I haven't heard from him for several days and was wondering if you know whether he's OK."

"Why, hello, Katie! Come on in, child. I'll be right down." A wave of apprehension at Mrs. McNamara's evasive answer swept over her. Stepping quickly up the stone steps and into the well-kept apartment building, she could hear the landlady's heavy footsteps descending the stairs. Katie's heart pounded from nervousness. At least she knew that whatever Mrs. "Mac" said would be the unvarnished truth.

"Would you like some hot coffee, Katie?" the motherly voice crooned as she approached with her slight limp. "That winter chill is already starting to close in. Here, let's sit down on the couch."

"Oh, no thank you, Mrs. McNamara. No coffee." Katie perched gingerly on the edge of the worn cushion. "I just want to know anything you can tell me about Fredrick. Is he OK? Do you know where he is? When will he be back? I really need to talk to him right away." Katie knew she was speaking too fast.

A long, awkward silence hung in the air as the older woman smoothed her gingham apron across her lap. "Well, my dear, I hate to be the one to tell you," Mrs. McNamara said slowly, looking first at the clock and then at Katie's tense face.

"Fredrick left in a really big hurry last week and said . . ." The older woman paused and blotted her forehead with a plain white handkerchief before continuing. "Well, Katie, he said he would not be back." She blurted out the words much the way a nurse pulls a bandage—matter-of-factly and quickly, so as not to hurt so badly. "He said he had been called to his home in Vienna, Austria, on an emergency. Didn't even bother about his furniture—told me to keep everything he left behind. All he took were his clothes, and poof, he was gone. I'm sorry—I thought you knew."

Tears welled up in Katie's blue eyes and for a while she could only swallow. Finally, she almost whispered, "Do you have an address?"

"No, my dear, I don't. Really didn't think to ask, since he had paid all his rent. I'm so sorry." She patted Katie's knee. "Men can sometimes be fickle, you know."

Katie knew Mrs. McNamara was trying to help, but the older woman could not possibly understand her predicament, and 23-year-old Katie couldn't explain, not now.

"Thank you," she murmured, brushing a hand across her eyes. Then, almost rudely, she rose to leave. In her stunned state of mind, the front door seemed miles away. She was glad Mrs. McNamara didn't follow.

Fredrick had been such a gentleman. She could not believe he was gone. Soon after she had arrived from New York a few years ago, penniless, scared, an 18-year old German immigrant, Fredrick Roess had befriended her. Having been in the country several years already, he knew the American customs, language, and where to apply for work. His English was perfect, and he had offered to show Katie around. He helped her find work and a place to live. They became friends quickly, and before long the friendship blossomed into love.

Now Katie stood and dried her tears. She slowly started toward her lonely third-story flat. Her long blond hair mercifully hid the swollen eyes that seemed riveted to the sidewalk. A wave of nausea swept over her, and the biting November wind didn't help. Fredrick had not given her the slightest clue that he was leaving the United States. But in her heart, of course, she knew why. On their last walk through their favorite park, she had told Fredrick the news. He seemed to have taken it extremely well. They had gone to his apartment to discuss over coffee what to do about it. Of course, he had agreed that if she truly was pregnant, they must get married, and right away.

Together they had set the wedding date, and he had given her money to buy an appropriate dress, one she could wear later. He didn't want a church wedding, which she preferred, but they had agreed together to simply go to the courthouse.

Fredrick's continual reassurances had fully convinced her of his happiness that they were to have a child of their own, a product of the love they had found together through those happy months. When he walked Katie home, he had held her close and repeated again how much he loved her, and how he looked forward to the day when they would share their love with their very own child. Back in her own apartment that evening, she had written her parents in glowing language of the upcoming wedding, telling anew of all Fredrick's wonderful qualities.

But now . . . she might just as well face the facts. He had left absolutely no trace. Anger, disappointment, and bitterness washed over her in successive waves. Maybe it was hatred she felt—or was it love? What *was* it? How could he have stolen her innocence and then fled all responsibility? How could he have pretended to be so dependable, so responsible, so kind? In spite of everything, Katie knew she still loved him. After all, he had helped her dream that someday they—she—would escape the hardships and poverty they had known for so long. Now what would she do? How could she possibly support a baby alone? What would she tell her parents back in Germany? With five children still at home to feed and clothe, they were certainly in no position to help her. Their impoverished state was one reason Katie had come to America.

Well, first she would have to forget any romantic notions and dreams of carefree days. German logic demanded that she quit grieving and take stock of her situation. Fredrick had been, without question, an absolute scoundrel. Katie determined to simply erase him from her memory. She would not even think of him, but would simply work her 12-hour shift at the bakery, and consider the tiny life growing inside her—how she would raise a child, how she would manage totally and completely alone.

But whenever a tall, handsome man passed the shop window, her heart still gave a momentary lurch until she realized it was not Fredrick. How *could* she forget him?

Katie knew her situation would grow more difficult as her predicament became obvious. A few days later at lunch, Helen, one of her coworkers, remarked, "Remember Ruth Damono who worked here a few months ago? She just had a baby—what a slut! I doubt she even knows who the father is." An audible gasp came from the others. Katie cringed inwardly. The nauseous spells were hard enough to hide, not to mention the weight gain and expanding waistline that Katie knew would soon be her lot. She could see that clothes would play a key role in hiding or revealing her condition, in addition to maintaining her dignity and perhaps even her job.

Katie recalled a trick she had heard her mother and aunt discuss back in Germany about making and wearing maternity dresses. A distant relative had become pregnant while working as a secretary for a large company. Though she was married and had no reason to be ashamed to be seen in public, it was well known that working women who got pregnant were usually fired. So she had skillfully and gradually padded her bosom so it always protruded farther than her abdomen. Except for appearing to have gained excessive weight, it greatly delayed the moment of truth.

So Katie took the wedding dress money Fredrick had given her and bought material, copying her distant cousin's clever idea. Since she had no sewing machine, she had to make every painstaking stitch of her new wardrobe by hand at night after a long shift at the bakery. Tears washed every garment before it was worn, but they were not tears of self-pity, nor even of humiliation. "How could I have been so *stupid* to get in this situation with only *talk* of marriage?" she remonstrated with herself.

It was a mixed blessing that her brother Jack soon arrived in Chicago from Germany. Although she was so busy she hardly had time to see him, she still valued and sought his understanding.

Life at the bakery did indeed become more difficult. Finally one day the shop's owner called her into the office. Katie was panic-stricken. She knew what to expect. If she lost her job, what would she do? No one would hire her in "that condition." The manager spoke softly but intensely.

"Katie," she said, "I never expected this of you. You always seemed so dependable and in control of yourself."

The girl made no excuses. She couldn't explain how Fredrick had treated her so wonderfully. Tears silently spilled down her face as she realized that no one cared or could understand how she had been utterly taken in with a promise of marriage, only to be totally deserted and left alone.

"You will have to be able to carry your share of the workload," her manager continued. "I cannot give you any time off. Business is business and must go on, regardless of predicaments that people get themselves into. I simply cannot give you any privileges the others don't have, especially when they find out you are going to have an illegitimate child."

The words stung like a scorpion. "I'll do my best, Mrs. Willingham," Katie sobbed. "I don't want to cause any problem for you. I'll be ever so grateful if you'll just let me continue my job."

When she walked back into the workroom, Katie felt the eyes of the other girls following her everywhere she went.

She began to think of how a wedding band would help to protect her from harsh looks and stinging comments, but that would be deceitful. Katie was far too honest—and too poor—to stoop to that. None of the customers would know the difference, but somehow she could not bring herself to do it. Once or twice she turned her gold birthstone ring so it appeared to be a wedding band, but then decided that was too much like lying. In Germany wedding bands were sacred. There, none but the lowest class would wear a wedding band if a woman was not married.

Chapter Two

Early Years

The months flew by quicker than Katie could have imagined. Somewhere along the way, her motherly instincts took over, and she became excited over the new life she felt stirring in her own body. She mustered up courage to write her parents back in Germany about their expected grandchild. After her own wardrobe was adequate, Katie began knitting and sewing tiny sweaters and dresses for her baby. Would it be a girl or a boy? What would she name her? Or would it be a him? A girl probably would be easier for a single mother to raise, she mused.

If it's a boy, will he look or act like his father? "No!" she determined stoically. "This boy, if it is a boy, will be of much finer stuff than his dubious father. He *could*—since he would be born in America—become president!" Even she had to smile at her motherly dreams.

Being of strong conscience, Katie eventually went to the priest and confessed her sin. His response was an unexpected comfort she often repeated to herself. "There are no illegitimate babies, Katie," he said gently, "only illegitimate parents." He also assured her of God's forgiveness if she would only bring the baby to the church to be baptized after it was born.

June was unusually hot that year, and Katie's tiny attic apartment was nearly suffocating to someone nine months pregnant. When labor started, Katie managed to walk down the two flights of stairs and call to the landlord's son. "Bobby," she gasped, "I think you'd better go and get Mrs. Whittaker." It was all she could do to stagger back up to her apartment. She hoped Bobby remembered where the midwife lived. The heat had drained her long before the labor became serious.

It seemed like hours before Katie heard lumbering steps slowly ascending the hot metal stairs, accompanied by what sounded like disgruntled muttering. Entering the room, Mrs. Whittaker acknowledged the perspiring mother-to-be with a cursory nod and removed her hat with its long sharp pin. Methodically, she opened her bag and laid out its contents. Boiling water hardly seemed necessary, since the tap water was so warm. "Whew!" she kept repeating as she mopped her brow. She did her job mechanically, almost without communicating. Soon the tiny baby arrived, red and screaming.

"A boy! A beautiful baby boy!" Motherly pride filled Katie's whisper when the midwife placed the little bundle in her arms. She hardly noticed Mrs. Whittaker's disapproving mumble. Katie put her finger against the flailing fist, and the little tyke wrapped his tiny red fingers around it. "Precious!" she whispered. "My precious little boy!"

The midwife didn't answer, but turned to wash her hands as soon as the new mother was reasonably comfortable. Katie had been able to squirrel away the three-dollar fee that she now pulled from under the mattress and weakly held out to Mrs. Whittaker. "Thank you for coming," she whispered.

The midwife accepted the money with a "Hmmph!" Then she spoke her first full sentence since arriving. "And what have you decided to name the little bastard?"

Devastated, Katie clutched the soft bundle to her face and shared his little yellow blanket to catch the unbidden flood of tears. She could not, would not, look up, but wrapped her arms protectively around the tiny infant as if to shield him from further insult. Sternly, the midwife stood over the sobbing mother for a moment, but realizing she would get no answer, finally turned, pinned on her hat, took up her worn bag, and left with a sigh, noisily wiping her feet outside the door.

It was hours before Katie's tears subsided. How could anyone condemn a tiny innocent baby? She had endured almost continuous insinuations in glances and comments, but it was hardly fair to have such insults directed against her child. It was almost more than she could take.

Katie realized, however, that tears would not solve anything, and she pulled strength from some unknown source to begin caring for her helpless infant, whom she now loved with all her heart.

During the next few days while Katie remained home, she began to worry about an even more substantive issue: who would keep the baby while she worked? She must find someone that week since she would return to her job on Monday. As she lifted the squirming infant from his clothes basket bed, she crooned and rocked him in her arms. "How can I give you up for 12 hours a day? Please understand that I must work so you can have what you need. There's no other way we can manage, my dear little guy!"

Katie asked the landlord if she knew anyone who would watch her baby. She also stiffly descended the apartment stairs to search the newspapers, to review the posting board at the grocery store, and then to inquire of the neighbors. It seemed no one wanted to keep a fatherless little waif, as if they were fearful of becoming contaminated by him. Finally, taking advantage of the young mother's desperate plight, an acquaintance of a neighbor agreed to keep him—at a greatly inflated price. Katie had no choice but to accept the offer.

Once back at work, Katie lived for Sundays. It was the one special day when she had her baby all to herself. Her first duty was to fulfill the vow she had made to the priest. She dressed her infant in the white hand-embroidered christening gown she had carefully crafted and took him to the large Catholic church nearby. Her brother would now become the child's godfather.

The priest shook the censers and chanted, and incense filled the air. When he asked the baby's name, Katie proudly answered, "Jack, after his uncle Jack, and his middle name is John, after my father." When the christening water touched Jack John's head, he objected lustily as if resisting the double name as well as all the attention.

The next few months were difficult for Katie and her child. Competent baby-sitters were hard to find, in spite of the Great Depression, which struck in the fall. As soon as Katie thought she had a good one, some crisis would arise, and she would have to start looking for another. No one wanted to keep "that kind of child." Sometimes she fell behind in the rent and was asked to leave. Unendingly, she searched the newspaper for cheaper or cleaner quarters, but the two criteria didn't seem to go together. Katie's own impeccable cleanliness contrasted sharply with that of most of her neighbors, wherever she lived.

One day she was pleased to discover a nice family in a more affluent neighborhood who were willing to keep her growing tot. Now she wouldn't have to worry. Even though she couldn't afford to live in those apartments, at least Jack could spend his long days away from her in a clean, comfortable, and loving home.

But then Katie began to notice that Jack, already slender, appeared to be getting thinner. Every evening when she entered the family's apartment to pick him up, he seemed unusually happy to see her. He always had a ravenous appetite when he got home, even though the family he stayed with had eaten shortly before she arrived. Katie worried that he might be getting some terrible illness.

Finally she asked Mrs. Moore, "Do you have any idea why Jack would be losing weight?"

Mrs. Moore answered in surprise, "Why, no, I hadn't noticed. He doesn't seem to eat much at our house. Must be he misses his mama. And of course, he is *very* active at his age."

One day work was slow at the bakery, and Katie left early.

When she arrived to pick up her child, she could see through the window that the Moores were eating supper. She could also hear Jack crying. Quietly she pushed open the door, only to see her hungry son sitting on the floor, crying and begging for food.

Mrs. Moore was saying sharply, "Shut up, Jack! Your mother will feed you when you get home."

Katie's heart sank. *So that's why he is so thin—they probably don't let him have lunch either.*

Later Katie found a family who did seem to love her son and treated him as one of their own. For several months everything went well, and Katie breathed a sigh of relief that Jack appeared to be a thriving and happy 2-year-old.

But one evening as Katie started up the stairs to the sitter's third-floor apartment, she heard a piercing scream. Instinctively, she knew something terrible had happened to Jack, and she literally flew the rest of the way up the stairs and burst into the sitter's apartment. Katie caught snatches of phrases as she rushed with the family out onto the balcony. "Wandered out there . . ."

"Pulled on broom handle . . ."

" . . . fell through the balcony slats . . ."

"Hurry!"

Sure enough, as Katie stumbled wildly, frantically, down the stairs, she learned that Jack had fallen from his sitter's third-floor balcony. When she reached his motionless body, blood was gushing from his head. Stunned and weak herself, Katie sank to the grass beside him, mumbling, praying, nauseated. Neighbors brought clean rags to soak up the blood. Someone drove them to the hospital, but little Jack had been seriously injured. It would be a miracle if he survived. Before morning his head had swollen to twice its normal size. Katie kept a 24-hour vigil beside his bed, refusing to leave until, at last, his vital signs stabilized and he began to recover.

"Mama!" he whimpered pitifully one morning. It was the most

beautiful sound Katie had ever heard. Miraculously, he did survive. And Katie marveled. Such a fall could easily have killed her son. An overwhelming feeling that God had spared Jack absorbed her. Did He have some special purpose in mind for her son? Perhaps he would someday be a priest. She would be sure to remind him of this miracle when he was old enough to understand.

Katie had to get back to the bakery. It would take a lot of overtime to make up for all the time she had missed. Fully convinced of God's hand in her son's miraculous recovery, she became more faithful than ever in attending mass and confession. She watched with increasing pride as her toddler grew, but she also realized that she would never be able to provide for their increasing needs all alone.

It was a happy day when a relative in a better area of Chicago, upon learning of Katie's predicament, opened her heart and home to them. Katie was ecstatic—and extremely grateful. Now Jack would have a chance to grow up away from the slum neighborhoods. Aunt Elke's children were much older, but they welcomed Jack as a new younger brother. Katie felt her prayers to the virgin Mary actually were being heard and answered.

Their presence in their new home, only a small apartment, no doubt crowded the original occupants, but to Jack and his mother it seemed spacious, immaculate, and filled with love, food, and laughter.

When it was time to start first grade, Jack, of course, went to the Catholic school around the corner. His teachers were dedicated nuns who loved all the children, and it seemed they loved Jack in particular. Perhaps the fatherless child especially touched their hearts. Jack soaked up their every attention.

One of the sisters pulled Katie and Aunt Elke aside at a school program one evening and asked a peculiar question. "I don't want to embarrass anyone, but I was wondering if there is a problem that you really cannot afford to give Jack breakfast before he comes to school?"

"Jack eats breakfast at home *every* morning," Katie answered indignantly. "What do you mean?" The color rose in her neck.

"Well," the nun explained, "whenever we ask, 'How many came to school without breakfast?' Jack almost always raises his hand. So we let him go with all the other hungry children for milk and graham crackers with the sisters."

Katie felt extremely embarrassed. Later she asked her son, "Why do you tell your teacher you're hungry in the morning when you eat a good breakfast every day?"

"Why, Mother, I never eat *much* breakfast at home because I want to go and sit next to the sisters," the boy answered innocently. "They're so nice."

Even though Jack received no more graham crackers and milk at school, he cleverly found many ways to be near the sisters and absorb their loving attention. While he was always treated with love and kindness at home, he was starved for affection during the long days his mother had to be at work. The nuns' devoted attention to him prompted a loving response to the church in which he received such compassionate treatment.

Chapter Three

The Farm

"Guess what!" Katie fairly shouted as she burst through the front door. "We're going to Germany!"

In the kitchen Aunt Elke hardly paused from turning the browned sausage into the steaming pot of sauerkraut. "Katie, that's great!" she sang out, knowing her niece had been saving every nickel possible for such a trip ever since moving in with them.

But it was a totally new concept to 8-year-old Jack. Mother grabbed him and whirled him in a happy dance around the room. "Isn't it wonderful!" she cried. "We're going to Germany! Aren't you excited, Jack?"

"Yeah, er, yes, I guess so," the boy stammered. He could tell from his mother's shining eyes and expectant smile that he should share her exuberance, but it would take a few minutes for him to grasp such news for the first time. Of course, the letters from Grandmother had always said they would love to see them, but Jack had considered that an impossibility. *Leave merry Aunt Elke and Uncle Rolfe?* he quietly thought to himself. They'd had so much fun as a family. Leave his cousins, Heidi and Frank? Leave the good food, the nearby park where he played, his beloved schoolmates, teachers, and friends? Why, he couldn't even speak German. What was Mother getting them into?

"Oh, Jack," she told him excitedly, "you'll get to see where I grew up! You'll *love* the farm. There's so many fun things to do—milk the cows, harness the horses to the wagon, plow with the oxen, harvest the summer hay—Grandfather has lots of animals, and a barn and fields and woods and streams." She gestured wildly as she spoke. "And Grandmother cooks wonderful food. Like Aunt Elke," she added quickly.

"I don't know, Mother," Jack answered slowly. "I like it here with Aunt Elke and Uncle Rolfe. How long will we be gone? What if I don't like it there?"

Mother dropped to the couch and pulled Jack down close beside her. "We'll have only two short months. The bakery is letting me off, but since I won't get any pay, we'll have to come back in two months so I can get back to work. You'll love Grandmother and Grandfather—they want to see you so badly. And you'll have so much fun, Jack, that you may not even want to come back home!" She laughed and hugged him reassuringly.

That evening they began a frantic flurry of preparation for their departure. Taking out the two battered steamer trunks she had brought on the ship from Germany, Katie Kiesling began packing everything they would need.

"The last time I used these old trunks," she told Jack, "I had to ride with them in the baggage compartment because I couldn't afford a real ticket. But this time we're going to ride in class! Well, *third* class, but at least we'll be considered passengers and not cargo!" Mother seemed more excited every time she came home from work.

A few weeks later she came flying through the door again, holding the tickets in her hand.

"We really are going home, Jack! We're going home!" she almost shrieked with delight.

The boy, however, still felt that Aunt Elke's house with its warm and wonderful smells, the cheerful, loving way the family treated each other, and his teasing but fun-loving cousins—*that* was home. At first he really had to try hard to be as excited as Mother, but soon he too began to actually look forward to the trip.

Time sprouted wings, and before long they were loading their trunks into a cab for the ride to the train station. When he saw the huge steam engine puffing into the station, Jack was even more excited than his mother. He had always wanted to ride the train. The long trip to New York left him enraptured at each new sight.

"Look, Mother, at those huge fields and all the cows! Is this what Grandfather's farm looks like?" The questions tumbled out. "Does just one family live in those huge houses on those big farms? Is that one like Grandfather's house?"

She laughed at her son's wide eyes and many questions. They were already having a grand trip, and it had hardly begun.

"Well, Jack," she explained, "not everyone in the world has to live in an apartment like we do. Grandfather's farm isn't nearly as big as one of these American farms, but he and Grandmother do have a big house where they live with their youngest children. Their fields are smaller, so their neighbors live closer than these farm neighbors do."

"That's even better," Jack decided. Picturing himself exploring the barn, riding a big horse, wading across a rocky creek, he could hardly wait to get there.

"Mother, are there mountains near Grandfather's farm?" Jack asked.

"No, there aren't any mountains close to the farm, but the land rolls gently into little hills, and it's green and beautiful."

"If there were mountains, I could climb to the top and look a hundred miles away. Or I'd look for caves and climb rocks or . . ."

His mother laughed, "You'll have more to do than explore mountains, Jack. Grandfather is expecting you to help him on the farm this summer. The months will fly by, and before you know it we'll be back in Chicago."

When they arrived in New York City, the raw squalor overwhelmed the boy. Tall, ugly gray buildings stretched high into the sky, blocking the sun from view. The streets were noisy, smelly, and dirty. It seemed everyone was rude and in a hurry. Mother and Jack caught a taxi to the pier. The boy tried to take in the sights from his seat by the window, but all he could see were dirty tenements with trash and filth of every description littering the street.

"This makes Chicago look pretty good, doesn't it?" he grinned. "How can people *live* like this?"

The cab driver added to the confusion by careening around corners, blaring his horn, yelling at pedestrians, and cursing at other drivers. The elevated cars roared past and street vendors squawked and hawked their goods. It was a relief when Katie and Jack at last reached the pier and boarded their steamer.

"Now *this* is a vacation!" she announced as soon as the ship left the pier. She lounged in a deck chair for days, always with a book in her lap, but almost always with her eyes closed. In the nearly 16 years she had been in America, it was her first real vacation. Oh, she had had some time off in the summers, but she could never afford to take Jack anywhere except on a streetcar ride to the lakefront beach. And though she always took advantage of any time off to sew or clean or even sleep late a couple times, she never seemed to have enough money to do anything else.

Now she would enjoy every minute of the eight-day trip. It was luxurious to go to the dining room and eat whatever she wanted, knowing someone else would prepare it, serve it, and wash the dishes. Jack had never seen his mother so relaxed and carefree. At night they would often stand by the railing and watch the stars appear. They loved the shimmering path the moon made across the ocean waves and the salty spray of the evening wind on their faces. In those evening moments Jack learned a lot about his mother—her dreams, her disappointments, her courage, her earlier life.

During the day Jack made friends with other children, and something was always going on in the playroom. Occasionally the boys played hide-and-seek on the deck, and sometimes

Jack just walked around exploring the ship, asking questions and making friends with the deck hands. About halfway across the ocean, Jack, dressed in a white sailor suit Aunt Elke had carefully stitched for their trip, went up to the navigation room to watch the captain guide the ship.

All too soon the voyage ended, and Jack and his mother found themselves on a train headed for southern Germany and Grandfather's farm.

"Look at how different everything is!" Jack couldn't keep from pointing and exclaiming at every new sight. The hills were smaller in Germany than he had imagined, and the fields were more the size of large gardens in America. Some of the houses looked funny, closely hugging the earth, their wide roofs drooping like Mexican sombrero rims. A number of farms had stone walls around them, with the house and outbuildings joined together. Church towers rose above every village, and red tile roofs clustered together in town as if seeking protection. The streets seemed narrow, and Jack didn't think he would want to live there. But when they went through a city, without exception, he was impressed with its cleanliness. These cities were not like Chicago, and certainly not like the parts of New York City they had seen. "Every family," his mother explained, "tries to keep the sidewalk in front of their home or business swept every day."

Soon their train left the cities behind, and luxuriant green hills appeared toward distant Bavaria. Lush green fields and trees contrasted with the brilliant blue sky. His head whirled from having seen so many new things. Everything was different from what he was used to—the trains, the stations, what people wore, and even the people, not to mention the language. Jack was glad his mother could understand and speak German. He was also thankful for the few words she had taught him on the ship.

The wooden bench in the third-class compartment of the train wasn't really comfortable, but the train car certainly was clean. Other people had thought to bring huge picnic baskets packed with bread, hunks of cheese, and fat sausages.

"Jack," Mother said apologetically, "I'm so sorry I forgot that we would not be able to get food on the train. Try not to look so hungry!" she laughed. A kind matronly housewife eventually offered a bit of her store to Jack, and Katie gratefully and apologetically accepted for him.

Everyone in the train car knew that she was going home, for she was too excited to hide it. Her eyes hardly left the window, even to check on Jack. She pointed out first one place she recognized, then another.

Finally the train pulled into their stop, and Mother spotted Grandmother and Grandfather Kiesling standing on the station platform, impatiently scanning the train cars. Jack and his mother scurried off the train, and before he could even look up, his grandmother swept him up in a hug. "*Ach, du liebes, armes Kind!*" she exclaimed, and she kept repeating it. Mother explained that Grandmother was saying, "Oh, you poor, dear child!"

"*Ein schönes Kind!* [A handsome child!]" Grandfather commented. Mother was crying and laughing and hugging, and then she remembered to properly introduce Jack, pointing out with pride and dignity that he was very much a member of their family because he had their name—Kiesling—and not his father's name.

"Isn't he kind of small for his age?" Grandfather asked in German.

"Have you been getting enough to eat?" Grandmother immediately chimed in. "Come, let's get into the wagon. We'll go home and get you a little something. You both are probably hungry after such a long trip."

Jack pictured a hot drink and some cookies or cake for a snack. But when he entered Grandmother's little kitchen, sausage, huge hunks of cheese, great loaves of black bread, and a whole crock of freshly churned butter covered the table. Mother's 14-year-old sister, Connie, served a wondrous Wiener schnitzel on each plate. Snowy mountains of mashed potatoes, tender homemade noodles, glistening red beets, garden-ripe tomatoes, thick sour cream—Jack lost track of the dishes. His eyes wanted to try everything. "I think I'm going to like it here," he whispered to his mother.

As they sat around the heavily laden table, Grandmother's joy at having her eldest daughter home was obvious. Throughout the lengthy meal everyone seemed to talk at once. Jack could understand an occasional word and knew they were speaking of each of Grandmother's children—the five boys and two living girls. (One girl had died as an infant in a tragic wagon accident.) Mother's brother Jack had gone to America when she was expecting her child. The two youngest children, Joseph and Connie, had been born after Katie had left home 16 years before, and they were still at home, along with 19-year-old Fritz, who had been just a toddler when Katie had left. They were all so happy to be together again that it seemed to Jack they talked forever, and Mother didn't have time to interpret for him everything they said.

Then it was time for dessert and coffee. Jack groaned, rolled his eyes, and held his stomach. The family laughed. Fritz, the oldest child at home, stood to his feet and motioned for Jack to go with him out to the barn. Grandfather's flock of geese set up quite a honking as they walked past. They seemed to want to peck at Jack, who eyed them uncertainly. He also noticed the chicken pen filled with plump hens and a rooster that strutted around his domain, bragging with an occasional lusty crow. Never before had the boy seen real live chickens. He could hardly believe they were a sample of what he had been eating throughout his brief life. The creatures had actually run around on two legs before finding their way to his plate. The pigs grunted, squealed, and pushed as they fought for food. Next was the calf pen, enclosing two wide-eyed calves, gentle and trusting in nature.

Inside the barn, tied in their milking stalls, cows contentedly chewed their cuds. All the creatures, even the old barn cat, amused and delighted the lad. Fritz lifted the three-legged stool from its peg on the wall, sat down beside a cow, and began to milk her. Jack knelt beside him and watched wide-eyed as liquid white streams filled the pail and a frothy foam formed on top. "So that's how they make milk!" he exclaimed to himself.

Jack was so fascinated with each new sight, sound, and smell that he scarcely noticed Mother entering the barn. "Curious Jack," her familiar voice held laughter, "you are such a sight in the barn in your very best clothes. You must go back to the house and change. Then you can watch Uncle Fritz do the rest of the barn chores."

It had never been so hard to obey promptly, but Jack never questioned his mother's no-nonsense approach toward doing what he was told. Obediently, he scurried back to the house with her, quickly changed his clothes, and eagerly rushed back to the barn to see what else might be going on. The entire afternoon was one adventure after another as Uncle Fritz patiently tried to explain everything he was doing.

All too soon their first day there ended, and when Mother called Jack to bed that evening, he realized how totally exhausted he was. Grandmother came to tuck him in under the feather comforter, with another hug and kiss to let him know how happy she and Grandfather were to have him there. Mother lingered a long time beside his bed, telling him about when she was a little girl and it had been her room. Back in Chicago she never had time to tell stories or even talk much to him, so he had known very little about her childhood. Now he could identify with every incident she mentioned, and her stories had genuine meaning.

Finally, with Mother's gentle voice in his ear, he fell asleep. A sense of belonging to his mother's family totally enveloped him.

Every day he learned the pronunciation and meaning of several new German words. Everybody talked so much that in almost no time he was able to carry on a conversation. *"Die*

Rinder pflügen das Feld [The oxen plow the field]." *"Die Kühe müssen gemolken werden* [The cows need milking]." *"Wasch deine Hände* [Wash your hands]."

Grandfather Kiesling took a special interest in being the father his grandson had never had. The boy became almost a shadow to him and Uncle Fritz. Jack liked to observe them as they hitched the big lumbering oxen to the plow. He faithfully followed the huge beasts through the field, watching their strong bodies respond obediently to Grandfather's grunts and crackling whip. After the older man turned the large, docile creatures loose in the barnyard, the boy would hand-feed them hay and feel their soft nuzzles as he scratched their noses.

By late summer his grandparents permitted Jack to go with the boys to cut hay. He was still too young and small to use the hand scythe that his tall, muscular young uncles did, but sometimes they would let him try. Jack loved the smell of freshly cut hay. He helped turn the hay with a big rake so it would dry thoroughly and be ready to stack, and he learned to pitch it onto the wagons that would take it to the barn for winter storage. The boy often rode on the hay wagon or sometimes on the back of one of those huge and intriguing oxen.

The days flew by, and Jack remembered that he had not yet chased rabbits or roamed the fields and streams as Mother had earlier suggested. After harvesting the early crops and scything the hay, it was time to gather the wheat and other grains into shocks. They beat the shocks by hand with special metal whips to release, or thresh, the kernels. Winnowing followed, accomplished with a hand-cranked fan that helped separate the chaff from the grain.

Soon Mother began talking about heading back to Chicago. Jack could hardly believe it was almost time to leave his beloved grandparents and their wondrous farm. How could he stand to leave so soon?

Grandmother and Grandfather hinted that they would really love for him to stay with them for a year. At first Katie dismissed the idea totally. "It is special for you to offer, but how could I get along without Jack? He's the center of my life!"

"Just look how the youngster has already filled out," her father replied. "His wiry little body is starting to develop muscle. He will grow and get stronger a lot faster out here in the sunshine and fresh air than he will on the streets of Chicago. Besides, he could learn a lot about farming, which he seems to love." Almost as an afterthought, he added with a chuckle, "He might even be able to help me some!" Then Grandfather expounded on how superior he felt the German educational system was, which would also "put Jack ahead."

Katie thought it over. She realized that she could never give her son the kind of experiences he would receive on the farm. Chicago would have street gangs, liquor, and many other teenage problems. Here, he would be away from the allure of the big city. Maybe it would help give stability to his life. But was it the right thing to do?

"Jack," she said one morning, "what would *you* really like to do?"

"Oh, Mother, I want to stay here!" the boy immediately and enthusiastically responded. He loved the farm, his grandparents, and his young aunt and uncles. Here he never suffered any long, lonely days, because they all worked together. He could speak German fairly well now and was happier than he could ever remember being.

Mother's heart was in her throat at his quick answer. *Have I been that bad a mother that my boy no longer needs or wants me?* she questioned. Fighting back her tears, she resolved that whatever it took, she would do the thing that would be best for her son. Only her pillow and God would know the loneliness that already engulfed her. She had won victories over poverty, shame, loneliness, and fatigue, and she could handle this also. Finally she told her parents she would take them up on their offer.

"While Jack is here," she told her parents, "I'll work extra so when he comes home we can move to a better part of town.

Maybe I'll even be able to get a better job by then."

However, as his mother packed, Jack began to have second thoughts. "Why can't you just get a job here, and then we can all be together as one big family?" he asked. As the thought of the long separation from his mother more fully registered with him, he determined to be brave. In only a year he would be going home, so maybe it wouldn't be so bad. Like most other 9-year-olds, however, he didn't think a lot about the future.

The day Katie was to leave, the whole family piled into the wagon for the trip to town. Jack sat beside his mother, his hand clasping hers tightly. He had determined that he would not cry, so he was strangely silent. His mother, too, choked back her tears and said little. She was afraid speaking her thoughts would only make it harder for her son. They arrived at the station far too quickly.

When the train pulled in, Fritz got on, and Grandfather and Joseph handed Katie's luggage through the window to him. When they had stashed away the last bag, Katie thanked and embraced her parents, her brothers, and her sister.

Then she turned to Jack. Suddenly, he grabbed his mother's arm and clung, panic-stricken, to her. "I'm going, too, Mother," he said huskily but with intense resolve. She tried to pull away to board the train.

"No, Mother, I'm going with you!" Jack repeated loudly and emphatically. "I've changed my mind. I want to go with you. *Please!* Please don't leave me here!"

His mother stepped up onto the train steps and tried to shake Jack's grip. The conductor was calling "All aboard!" in German. She must go. Unable to speak and with tears streaming down her own cheeks, Katie let Grandfather and Fritz pry Jack's fingers loose. She scurried up to the platform at the end of the train car and turned to wave, then disappeared inside just as the train began to jolt forward. She reappeared at the window for one last glimpse of her kicking, screaming 9-year-old being forcefully held by her brothers. He had never behaved that way in his life, and it deeply troubled her. For many miles she cried, even though she knew Jack would be much better off there. A year would be gone before she knew it, and she would work hard so life would be better for them both after that.

But Jack could not be comforted. Even after his desperate rage subsided, he wailed miserably all the way home. Before leaving that morning, Grandmother had prepared his favorite meal, but when they got home, he could not or would not eat. Running upstairs, he flung himself into the feather comforter and mourned inconsolably.

"Come on, Jack," his uncles coaxed, "we need you to pat the cow's noses so they'll be calm while we milk them." But he refused to leave his bed.

Throughout the night he cried. Grandmother kept coming in to comfort him, but nothing she said or did helped. For three days and nights he lay there grieving and weeping. Every morning Grandmother came in and changed the wet pillows, hanging them over the windowsill to dry in the sun.

"How can one little body produce so many tears?" Grandfather asked again and again, obviously wondering whether they had made the right decision.

Finally, after three days of not eating and little sleep, exhaustion overcame Jack, and mercifully for all, he slept. When he awoke, his wise grandmother was beside his bed with warm broth and crusty black bread. She fed it to him as they talked about what had happened during the past few days.

Slowly his pain subsided, and Jack gradually began to enjoy the animals and the farmwork again. Now he determined to throw himself into the farm tasks so that when he would see his mother in Chicago in a year, she would be proud of him.

But neither of them knew what the next year held.

Chapter Four

Busy Days

Jack liked the farm, even his chores (which greatly increased as his strength increased), but he especially loved his relatives. They made him feel needed and useful, and Grandfather soon began to brag, "Why, Grandmother, I believe that Jack can do almost as much work as a man!" Fritz had been drafted into the German military shortly after Katie left, and since he was no longer there to help with the heavy chores, Grandfather's comment made Jack really feel grown up.

In mid-September Grandmother said, "Jack, it's time for us to get you enrolled in school." The next morning she walked with him to the elementary school in the village, a short distance from the farm. Since everyone in town was Catholic, the public school was essentially a Catholic one, and the boy felt right at home. The local priest came to the school and taught religion classes.

"Jack," the priest said one day, "you have been a very good boy in school, the sisters say, and your marks in my classes are very high. Would you like to serve God as an altar boy?"

"Oh, yes, Father," he responded eagerly. That meant that he studied Latin along with his other classes. Soon he could chant with the others, *"Hoc est Corpus Meum, Dominus Vobiscum."* Eventually he became head altar boy, pleasing his grandparents greatly.

Jack found the school year challenging, learning a new language in a new culture, with new family and new friends. At home he was extremely busy with schoolwork, as well as with all the farm chores. He never had a problem falling asleep. But the family greatly missed Fritz.

Almost before Jack knew it, the school year came to a close, and his June birthday would make him 10 years old. After celebrating with a great German meal and special games with the family, he began to think seriously about how soon it would be time to pack and head back to Chicago. Emotionally, he felt himself torn. His grandparents had lovingly given him the secure home he'd never had, but of course he longed to see his mother, to talk to her about all he had learned and to show her how much he had grown. He wanted more than anything for her to be proud of him. Every letter Katie wrote told how many days remained until they would be together again in mid-September and how much she missed him.

Jack was vaguely aware of a man named Adolf Hitler who had aggressively established total control over Germany, and who seemed to have ideas of conquering the world. His influence had spread quickly—if one could believe what one heard. However, the village grocery store contained the only radio found in the entire community, so the local citizens were relatively ignorant of what was happening in the rest of the world. (Besides having only one radio, the little farm village also had only one telephone, owned by the Bürgermeister, or mayor.) When something really important was announced on the radio, the grocer would share it with the Bürgermeister, who would then have the news proclaimed by the town's bell ringer.

Then on September 1, 1939, just days before Jack's scheduled departure, Hitler invaded Poland. With brutal and bloody suddenness, World War II began. No one could leave Germany openly. Jack was blissfully unaware of the outspoken opposition to Hitler that his grandfather had expressed a few years earlier. Nor did he know that Grandfather had ended up going to prison as a result. Because of that experience, his grandparents would not even consider trying to smuggle Jack out of the country. They didn't want to come under suspicion again. A trip to prison in peacetime was one thing, but under war circumstances, such foolishness could bring death. It was simply too risky for everyone concerned to chance trying to send Jack home to his mother. Besides, with Fritz already serving in the German army, the family really needed the boy to help on the farm.

So, instead of heading for New York and Chicago, Jack found himself back in the Catholic elementary school in the village. "Well, it probably will be only a couple months until the war ends," he told Grandfather, "so I might as well enjoy my time here."

The boy was smart enough to realize he should keep quiet about being an American, both in school and elsewhere. He trusted Grandfather implicitly and was happy on the farm, so he yielded willingly to the decision to remain in Germany. Mother's letters indicated that trust also, though she longed to see her son again.

"Jack," she wrote, "though I'd like nothing better than to see you soon, you're probably much safer on a peaceful farm in south Germany than on a ship that could be attacked by a German U-boat. I know you'll be a big help to Grandfather until you can come home."

"Soon the war will be over," Jack added to the letter Grandmother was writing to his mother, "and then I will head for Chicago."

But the war continued into winter and, unknown to Jack, fiercely gathered in intensity. Even in their little school students had to learn to salute with outstretched arm and say, *"Sieg Heil!"* The German Youth Movement became an integral part of the elementary school system. No one could escape the political indoctrination.

Through the uncertain source of the radio news reports, Grandfather discovered that the war was not only continuing, but was raging more furiously than any conflict in history. It had greatly distressed him when the government drafted Fritz, but he had not dared to speak his mind. Being a typical 10-year-old, Jack was not overly concerned about world affairs, though he did occasionally hear Grandfather and Grandmother talking quietly about Hitler, the war, and their sons.

A year passed. And more months. Jack found the Youth Movement greatly to his liking except for the strange Nazi salute. Nazi indoctrination for young boys reminded him of Boy Scouts—the various activities encouraged good sportsmanship, obedience to law, and respect for authority. He didn't realize that a subtle brainwashing was also taking place, designed to eliminate God and religion, and eventually to turn children against their parents. Oblivious to that, he began to feel quite important in his uniform. Everyone had a sense of identity and a certain importance, and he saw nothing wrong with that.

But Grandfather's family faced increasingly distressing days. Fritz had been drafted almost two years ago, and now, as he turned 18, Joseph had to enter military service. Jack would never forget the day. "Oh, Joseph, how can I let you go!" Grandmother wailed. He had been her favorite, and seeing the last son off to war was hard on the entire family.

After Joseph's basic training, he wrote home, "I'm being sent to the Russian front. Pray for me." Grandmother did not laugh easily after that, and the family often observed her whispering to herself and fingering her rosary.

Now Grandfather (in his sixties) and Grandmother had to run the farm, with only 15-year-old Connie, and Jack, not yet 11, to help. With no mechanized farm equipment, it was an overwhelming, if not impossible, task. Jack tried the best he could to take the heaviest of the farmwork, but Grandfather, though kind at play, was an even sterner taskmaster than before. He worked extremely hard himself, and he expected everyone else to do likewise, regardless of their age. The family had little now to joke about. Survival was the only thing that mattered.

One fateful Sunday morning the priest announced in a choked and tremulous voice, "Our church bells will be removed this week and melted down for munitions. After this week, the government will not look with favor on church worship. Our church will be closed."

The villagers bowed their heads in sorrow as they slowly made their way home after Mass, but no one dared speak their opinion. Throughout Germany church bells traditionally rang for every occasion—in joy at the wedding of a village couple, at the birth of a new baby, or when celebrating a golden anniversary or any other happy time. They also rang in sorrow—tolled for the death of an infant or any other citizen, for fallen sons or fathers in battle, or for a national tragedy. Every evening as the sun went down, the bells tolled the end of day. Every Sunday morning bells announced the day of rest and chimed a call to worship. The older people especially seemed to measure their lives by the ringing of church bells.

Jack, as head altar boy, had rung those bells himself many times. Holding firmly to the ropes, he would pull with all his weight and strength to get them swinging. To stop them, he grabbed the ropes and rode them high until his body weight finally brought them to a standstill again.

The boy and his grandfather were out in the field when the soldiers came for the bells. The villagers gathered to watch. They knew that the bell tower had purposely been erected first, then the church built around the tower so no one could easily steal the bells. To the soldiers, it appeared impossible to remove the bells without tearing down the whole church. They sweated and swore as they worked while townsfolk winked silently at each other. Finally, the soldiers decided to pound the bells to pieces. When they began hammering, the bells rang out rich and clear, sending their beautiful tones over the countryside for the last time. For hours the townspeople stood transfixed, listening for the last time to the melodic sounds. To Jack, their notes seemed to declare, "Never give up hope! God's love cannot be destroyed."

But for Grandfather the final toll of the bells was the sound of doom. Being a religious man, he seemed to physically feel each strike against the iron. From the corner of his eye, Jack could see the old man's weathered face visibly wince. Finally, there was a loud crack, and a tear escaped down Grandfather's dusty face as he stared in resignation toward the church. The largest bell had shattered. The soldiers removed it piece by piece from the tower. The smaller bells didn't take as long. As each bell cracked, Grandfather took off his hat, crossed himself, and said a prayer for the soldiers' forgiveness, thinking, no doubt, of his own soldier sons.

The soldiers finally finished their task, and a heavy silence hung over the valley.

Chapter Five

Dangerous Days

It's 4:00, Jack! Time to get up," Grandmother called. The boy climbed sleepily out of bed. The barn was always cold this time of day, but it seemed to warm up after he fed the cattle, cleaned up the night's manure, and milked the cows and goats. By the time he returned to the house, he was glad to sit down to a hurried but bountiful breakfast before heading off to school. After school every day throughout the summer, he worked hard in the fields, hoeing, plowing, haying, planting, reaping, or whatever had to be done. The work was exhausting, but he had no time for complaining or self-pity.

Every morning Jack scooped the manure from the barn and wheeled it out to the barnyard, where he dumped it in a big square pile, leaving the aromatic mess to "cure" so they could later use it as fertilizer. Early in the spring he would load every pitchforkful onto a wagon, take it to the fields, and unload it into many small piles. Then he came back to these small piles and spread them manually with a smaller pitchfork. Before they planted the crops, they had to plow the fertilizer into the ground to enrich the soil.

Felling trees from the edge of the forest opened new ground to plow in the spring. The farmers cut the trees with a crosscut saw with a man on each end (or in this case, one man and one boy). Grandfather took the best wood to the market to sell. The remainder he and Jack cut into firewood lengths and loaded onto the wagon. Then they hauled it to the backyard, where they stacked it in neat, almost artistic, piles. They even raked up the leaves to use for the animals' winter bedding. Of course, they had to remove all the stumps before they could plow the new land. These they laboriously dug up by hand, cutting the roots and digging until the stumps were loose enough to pull out either by hand or using the oxen.

The family wasted nothing—even splitting the stumps with wedges and sledgehammers to feed the potbellied stove for heating or the kitchen range for cooking. Their frugality paid off every winter. Naturally, though, the stove heated only rooms on the first floor. Many times during the winter when Jack awoke in his little room under the eaves, ice would be an inch thick on the window. It would have been fun to watch the sun come up and melt it into icy frescoes, but he had no time for such frivolous idleness. Life was serious, especially during the cold harsh winters, and no one could stop to enjoy the beauties of the season for long. They had cattle to feed, wagons to repair, and plows to make ready for spring.

Everyone slept on straw mattresses. Each spring and fall Grandmother replaced the straw with dusty-smelling new straw during housecleaning time. Of course, the farmhouse had no electricity or running water. The family took baths for only special occasions, especially in the winter. Everyone was always happy for the first warm days in late spring when they could go to the river for a bath. If someone needed a bath in the winter—for a wedding, for instance—then he or she had to pump water from the well, haul it to the house, and heat it on the kitchen stove. A large wooden washtub served as a bathtub, mixing hot water heated on the stove with cold water brought directly from the well.

Of course, the farm had no indoor toilets, only an outhouse. But a small chamber pot served for nighttime emergencies. On cold mornings Jack jumped out of bed and dressed very quickly.

In December 1941 the radio at the grocery store sputtered out a chilling announcement: "The Japanese have bombed two major U.S. military installations off the coast of Pearl Harbor, and thousands of U.S. soldiers are dead." Grandfather's face was drawn when he came home with the news. Wordlessly, he gave Jack a rare hug. Letters from Mother back in Chicago abruptly stopped coming. Instinctively, Jack knew they would have no more contact with her until the war ended. The United States was now unquestionably in the war, and Jack at age 12 could from this point on be considered an enemy of the Third Reich. But perhaps the government officials did not know his background.

Meanwhile, he had more pressing concerns. One of the physically hardest chores he had to work at was plowing new land behind the two strong oxen. The uneven ground was stony and full of roots. It was back-breaking, arm-wrenching work to try to hold the plow in the soil and keep the furrows straight, but he learned to lean his whole body on the plow while keeping his feet on the ground. It was good that he was growing so healthy and strong from constantly using every muscle.

Summers were incredibly busy. One day followed another so quickly that it was hard to realize how long he had actually been with Grandmother and Grandfather. Soon another school year began, to add to the busyness of his work life.

One day in late 1942 as the Battle of Stalingrad raged, Jack started home from the fields. Approaching town, he could hear women wailing, something that always took place when a father or son had died in the war. One could hear the sound a long way off as it echoed back from the hills. It sent chills racing up and down his spine. Jack knew that some really bad news had come through, either on the radio or by the postman. Perhaps another village friend had fallen.

As he neared home, he began to realize that the wailing was not coming from someone else's house, as had often been the case, but from his own. He hurried the oxen along, his heart sinking as he prayed. As he neared the farm, he could tell that the tragedy of war had indeed struck his house. It was Grandmother wailing. Quickly he tied the oxen, and as he approached the house, Grandfather strode heavily out the door, looking wild-eyed and drawn. Inside, Connie spoke softly to Jack, "Here's Joseph's wallet and ring. The government sent all his things from the battlefield of Stalingrad, along with the announcement that he was killed in action."

Grandmother and Grandfather were devastated. Jack saw before his very eyes what "heartbroken" meant. While stricken with loss himself, he knew the work could not stop. Even today's evening chores must be done. The family must somehow carry on.

Another birthday came and went for Jack, this time with no laughter or celebration. It was 1943, and Jack was 14 years old, now an elementary school graduate. He must decide whether he wanted to stay on the farm and become a farmer, go to a nearby trade school, or leave and prepare for the university and a profession.

Though Jack loved the farm and his grandparents, he knew he didn't want to spend his entire life there. The work was simply too brutal. "You know, Grandfather, what really appeals to me is to become an aeronautical engineer. I'd love to learn to fly."

Sadness overwhelmed his grandparents. If Jack went away to prepare for the university, they would have no one but Connie to help with the farmwork, and she could not do it alone. "I don't like that idea at all, Jack," Grandfather objected, "but if you want to fill out the application and send it in, I won't hold you back from your dream of a better life. It might keep you off the front lines should the war continue until you reach conscription age." Of course, it was impossible to consult with Mother on the matter, since all communication to and from the United States had ceased.

Jack had taken some classes in drafting and had done well, so he sent the forms in, answering honestly all the questions about age, nationality, place of birth, etc. Soon, to his delight, he received word from the government asking him to appear for schooling at Koenigswusterhausen on the outskirts of Berlin.

Grandfather and Grandmother sadly, reluctantly, took him to town and bought him some new school clothes and a train ticket. Grandmother, with wise forethought, carefully sewed a few hoarded deutsche marks into the lining of his jacket "for an emergency." In a matter of days, he was on his way with a brimming basket of food to sustain him on his journey. Little did he know the abrupt and drastic changes he was about to experience.

Chapter Six

Higher Education

When Jack reached Berlin, he got off the train. "How do I get to Koenigswusterhausen?" he asked the stationmaster. The man behind the counter raised one eyebrow and replied, "See that train on the far tracks? You need to get on that train. It will be leaving in about 20 minutes. It doesn't take long to get there."

Jack was eager to get to school and start his new classes. It would be his opportunity to show his mother and his grandparents how proud they could be of their aspiring aeronautical engineer. He might even become a pilot if the war continued. The full ramifications of exactly what that meant had not quite occurred to him as he boarded the last train to take him to his destination.

The boy was too excited to even sample the food Grandmother had so carefully packed for him. He dreamed of being at the head of his class—at least here he would not have to worry about schoolwork *plus* farmwork. Then he noticed that there were only a few people on the train. "Must be this school is only for the very select," Jack reasoned with a touch of pride. "I wonder if someone will be there to meet me?"

Sure enough, when he arrived and descended from the train onto the station platform, a tall young soldier in full military uniform, black boots, brown shirt, and a bold swastika on his arm waited. The stern-faced Nazi asked his name, then said, "Good. Come with me."

Picking up his suitcase, Jack followed, silently wondering if the aeronautical engineering preparatory school could also be a training institute for soldiers. They had walked about half a mile when, as they turned a corner in the road, Jack saw the barbed wire. A deathlike stillness hung in the air. Suddenly he realized that something was terribly wrong. An almost inaudible gasp escaped his lips, and all color drained from his face. His legs became very weak as a flood of disturbing thoughts flooded his mind. *This is not a school—this is a Nazi labor camp! And this is a Nazi guard leading me, like an idiot, into a labor camp!*

Sensing Jack's apprehension, the soldier quickly explained, "This is a screening place for all applicants to the engineering school."

But Jack knew better. The chilling realization of how he had innocently, even eagerly, walked into the trap almost made him ill. But there was no escape now.

Soon he learned that labor camps worked people to the point of exhaustion seven days a week with little food and few, if any, comforts until they collapsed or died. New "students" were always coming in to replace the fallen. However, labor camps were still a step above concentration camps. A concentration camp existed only to exterminate its inmates. With little food its inmates either died, were selected for medical experimentation, or were gassed and/or cremated, then buried in a mass grave.

How could I have been so gullible? Jack remonstrated with himself again and again. Of course, he realized that he was in the labor camp because he was an American citizen. He wondered if any ill fate had come to Grandmother, Grandfather, and Connie for harboring him. But he could not expect to write them or hear from them, perhaps ever again. Jack realized he was now totally alone, at age 14, in a hostile environment.

The labor camp housed all kinds of political prisoners from throughout Europe, including many from Germany. Since they were people the Reich dared not torture or gas, they did the next best thing—they worked them to death. A "natural" death was easy to explain to the International Red Cross, particularly with the food shortage. Besides, the government needed good cheap labor to keep the war effort going.

Jack now realized that the Hitler Youth Movement with its wonderful goals and activities had been simply a method of brainwashing the nation's youth. Remorse for his participation in it swept over him as he began to understand that Hitler was slaughtering all who dared to withstand him. The little village near Grandfather's farm had received essentially no news, and townspeople found it easy to believe what the radio proclaimed—that Hitler was the savior of the German people. Few had the courage to openly oppose the idea, including Grandfather. The sickening realization that an entire nation had been duped nearly overwhelmed Jack. He began to understand that the German government so tightly controlled the press, radio, and all other forms of communication that the people did not have a clue as to what was really going on. Suddenly he felt sorry for his innocent family and friends.

But he had little time to waste in sympathy for others, or for that matter, for himself. While Jack was accustomed to the 4:00 a.m. rising time to start work, he was not used to working all day on a nearly empty stomach. He began to dream of Grandmother's sausage and eggs, potato pancakes, and homemade black bread thick with jam and butter. The camp diet was bread and water with extremely little bread. But the water did help pacify the gnawing stomach pangs.

Bunks in the barracks were stacked four high, each with a thin straw tick thoroughly infested with cockroaches, lice, fleas, and other insects. Occasionally the guards sent the men to delousing centers and sprayed them with chemicals, but no one ever treated the bunks, so it did little good. Even in bitter subzero temperatures, they had only a light blanket for sleeping. Inmates learned quickly to sleep fully clothed, including overcoat and shoes, in order to survive. The acrid odor of unwashed human bodies permeated the barracks.

Winter came early that year. With the intense cold, the brutally hard work, and the near-starvation diet, Jack's once-strong body began to waste away. Sickness was rampant in the camp, and many political prisoners died a "natural and unfortunate death."

Whenever guards and officers had free time, they liked to taunt the prisoners. Boxing was a big thing around the world. Prior to the war, the Black American Joe Louis had defeated the German Max Schmelling, and the German guards had not forgotten or accepted it. Determined to prove the superiority of the German race, and particularly of themselves, they wanted to vindicate Max Schmelling. In their thinking, a Black American, someone whom they considered as grossly inferior to the German race, had humiliated the Aryan superrace. Never mind that Joe Louis had outfought all the supermen of his day.

One day the camp commandant announced, "Since all prisoners need entertainment and diversion from labor [despite the fact that they worked 12-hour days and their bodies begged for rest], we are going to divide you into weight classes and watch you box." A sinister sneer flickered across his face.

Boxing was the last thing the men wanted to do, but the guards promised the winners extra food, so everyone learned to do his best to defeat even friends. The "games" were designed to turn inmates against each other and contributed to the survival of the fittest mentality so prevalent in the camp. Officers and guards must be entertained, regardless of the cost. In a sense, every man and boy found himself forced into the ring to fight for his life.

Jack knew nothing about boxing. He had never worn a pair of boxing gloves in his life. But sooner or later everyone must take his turn. The camp commandant put Jack in the flyweight class—the lightest weight of all—because he was so small. When his turn to box came, he tried to confidently put on the gloves much as he put on an artificial air of hope. Since the winner was supposed to receive more food, he determined to be the winner. Somehow, miraculously, the scrappy little farm boy won. After a few fights, he became camp champion in his weight class, upsetting the commandant, particularly when the man discovered that the lad was an American. Now Jack must fight not only for more food and his own survival, but because he felt a moral obligation to defend the good name of his country and the reputation of Joe Louis.

Jack remained unbeaten in his weight class, so the commandant put him up against the champion of a heavier class. The youngster fought the best he knew how, but he could barely hold his own against the larger, older, stronger man. The contest dragged on and on. Since the older man seemed unable to knock Jack out, the camp commandant became infuriated. He decided to get into the ring himself and teach Jack a lesson. The stocky, well-fed, muscular Nazi officer attacked the half-starved, exhausted American boy. Jack had to fight back or the commandant would have become even more furious, so he did his best. No one dared cheer for him. The bout left Jack so savagely beaten about the head that it was a miracle that he did not sustain permanent brain damage.

Afterward, he remembered nothing except the brutal beginning. The commandant had unleashed his full wrath on Americans in general, and the unwilling audience thought they had witnessed a murder. Jack suffered from the beating for a long time. If Joe Louis had known how a desperately hungry young teen had nobly tried to defend his homeland and the Black American world champion, he would have been proud of the youngster.

By now the Allies were bombing Germany with a vengeance. Berlin came under almost constant attack. The labor camp ordered its inmates to construct dugouts that resembled earthen igloos, supported on the inside by boards and posts, then covered with about two feet of dirt. The igloo would not, of course, protect from a direct bomb attack, but it offered some protection from shrapnel and flying debris.

When air-raid sirens went off in the night, everyone would jump out of bed and rush to one of the igloo shelters. They would sit huddled inside for a couple hours until the bombing ended. From the explosions they could map out in their minds how close or far away the bombers were. "Less than a kilometer," someone might say, and the others silently nodded. They heard the heavy drone of Allied bombers flying over, then the piercing scream of their descending bombs. The earth rumbled and shook with every explosion. The men could then hear the chatter of machine guns as the German fighter planes attacked the bombers. Antiaircraft batteries from the ground tried to knock the American planes out of the sky. A long eerie silence usually followed the noise and confusion, indicating that the strike was over for the night.

Once after shivering in the dark air-raid shelter for hours, Jack and the others were just beginning to relax. The droning bombers had turned away from the city, with the German fighters in hot pursuit. Everyone was about to file out of the igloo, grateful for surviving another attack, when all of a sudden they heard a lone Allied bomber still coming toward them. Rushing back to their places, they waited and listened. Single bombs dropped methodically, spaced out along a path coming nearer and nearer, each explosion closer and louder, shaking the ground beneath them. Then a powerful bomb exploded only a few hundred yards away, sending dirt cascading down around their heads as the earth shook violently. Their ears popped from the pressure wave, while the posts holding up the dirt roof squeaked threateningly under the shifting load. The men sat silently, immobilized with fear, holding their breath while everything around them heaved and trembled. They somberly waited for the inevitable. The next bomb was certain death for them all.

But instead, they heard only silence—except for the fading

drone of the retreating plane and the *rat-a-tat-tat* of a chasing fighter. For a long moment no one spoke. Then the air-raid siren sounded the "all clear," and they jumped to their feet.

"That was close," one man said.

"I wish it had gotten us," another answered.

Without further comment, each man hurried back to his bunk to continue the fruitless effort to get warm under his one thin blanket.

The next morning the guards assigned Jack to clean up outside. Only then did he fully realize what a miraculous night they had experienced. The men observed the precision-like spacing between each bomb crater, the obvious target of each bomb, and the direction of the plane's path—unmistakable evidence that if the pilot had had one more bomb, it would have made a direct hit right on their shelter, and no one in that group would still be alive. Jack pondered the implications of that for a long time. Had providence once again stepped in to rescue him from certain death? Was this God's doing, or was it merely coincidence? And what about those who had not been so fortunate?

Jack thought about his uncle Joseph and how war had snuffed his young life out so soon after he had left to serve his country. He wondered about his grandparents. An intense longing to see them swept over him. Who knew what might have befallen their other two sons who were fighting the Americans?

Am I helping the Germans by being in this labor camp? Jack wondered. *Am I even an American after being in Germany so long?* The war left him torn and confused. He loved his uncles, his grandparents, his mother, and his American relatives, and he earnestly prayed that the virgin Mary would watch over each of them, wherever they were.

Chapter Seven

Escape

In winter the cold bit into his thin body until Jack's fingers stiffened and he thought he couldn't lift another log or stone. Nights were worse. He never got warm enough to sleep soundly. In summer the intense heat, unsanitary conditions, and insects made life miserable. Work in the labor camp fields was far more exhausting than it had ever been at Grandfather's farm. Lack of food left him dazed, and he had barely enough strength to walk, let alone work in the unrelenting heat. Every day was a survival test against harsh conditions.

Then one morning at roll call, the Nazi officer bellowed, "Jack Kiesling!" startling the boy out of his stuporlike state. The guard then read some other names and told them all to report to the commandant immediately. *This could only mean one thing,* Jack thought. *Well, death couldn't be any worse than life at the camp for all these many months.* He only wondered how they would do it.

Anxiety gripped the men and boys who wordlessly made their way to the office. Once inside, the commander announced that they were to be "relocated" to Leipzig to work in a munitions factory. A guard brought in their civilian clothes and dumped them unceremoniously on the floor. "Put these on!" he ordered.

After everyone had changed clothes, the entire group went by train to the work camp at Leipzig. For several days they waited around for uniforms to arrive so they could receive their assignments and begin orientation for their new jobs. It didn't take long for Jack to notice that the new camp was not as heavily guarded as their previous one.

Late one afternoon as Jack wandered around the compound near one of the factory warehouses, he decided on the spur of the moment to escape. Pressing his thin body against the wall of the building, he slithered along until he came to the corner. There he spotted a small hole in the bottom of the fence, and without thought of consequences, he raced to the fence, quickly wriggled through the hole, and started walking as nonchalantly as he could manage toward the railroad station. With the money Grandmother had hidden in his civilian clothes, he had just barely enough to buy a ticket to his grandparents' village. Doubtless all who saw him thought he was just a young German farm boy, for no one questioned him.

It was evening when Jack arrived at the farm, and Grandfather answered his knock at the door. When he saw his grandson, he stared in disbelief—seemingly immobilized. Then he quickly pulled the boy inside and hugged him tightly. Grandmother, wondering who could be knocking so late, also came to the parlor. When she saw Jack, she let out a little cry and then smothered him with kisses and hugs. They were overjoyed to know that he was alive. To Jack, it was wonderful to be free and home again. But his joy was extremely short-lived.

Grandfather immediately became serious. "You can't stay here," he said, actually trembling with fear. "If anyone finds out I am harboring an escapee from a labor camp, I could be sent there myself—or worse. It is too dangerous for all of us for you to stay here. As hard as it will be, I'm afraid you must turn yourself in."

His grandson could scarcely believe what he was hearing, but as he listened, Jack knew that what Grandfather said was true.

"Jack, you are *so* thin," Grandmother sympathized. "You must be very hungry. Let's see what we can find for you. Come to the kitchen so I can hear everything that has happened to you." She did all she could to feed him well.

It felt good to have a warm full stomach and to think of a comfortable place to sleep. After the meal, both Grandmother and Grandfather strongly advised Jack to go to the authorities first thing in the morning.

It was not easy to do, but Jack knew he must protect his grandparents, so the next morning he mustered up his courage and went straight into town to the police. He thought they would immediately send him back to the labor camp near Berlin or to the munitions factory in Leipzig. Instead, they sent him to a munitions factory farther south in Pegnitz near Nuremberg.

The large camp housed many kinds of people, carefully segregated by nationality, behind huge barbed-wire fences. The Germans purposely housed American, British, French, and Russian prisoners of war in one section of the huge compound to keep the Allies from bombing the factory. The authorities placed Jack in a section of the compound containing German political prisoners. Numerous displaced persons arrived daily from Poland and other occupied countries throughout Europe. They came in boxcars so jammed together that everyone had to stand upright. Germany needed the men and women to keep its war machines rolling since so many of its own citizens were on the front lines.

Routine for this camp was much the same as that at the first one except that the work was inside and extremely confining. Workers on either of the two 12-hour shifts had to stand in one spot in order to operate their machines. The camp assigned Jack to a lathe, where he had to make precision parts—for what, he did not know.

Everyone rose at 5:00 a.m. Breakfast consisted of one cup of black coffee and one slice of dry bread. After standing for six hours, it felt good to get out of the building and march to lunch, where they could sit down. Inmates had 30 minutes to eat one bowl of watery potato soup and two small slices of dry bread. It was easy to finish the meager rations in the allotted time. Then they worked again until 6:00. Supper consisted of a single cup of coffee and a single slice of dry bread. Then everyone spent more hours standing out in the yard listening to a daily indoctrination session broadcast over the loudspeaker. The limited diet, essentially bread and water, along with the hours of standing soon took its toll. Jack wasted away until he was as thin as a concentration camp victim, weighing only 80 pounds, which, even for his small frame, made him look like a hollow-eyed skeleton.

On holidays, especially around Christmas, Allied prisoners of war in adjoining camps received packages from home or from the Red Cross. Jack and his companions gathered at the fence and stared as those prisoners opened their packages and exclaimed over the contents. He noticed that American prisoners got the most and the largest packages. Russians got the fewest and the smallest. It didn't seem fair. What difference should it make what country one came from? Everyone was fighting the same enemy, and he thought the packages should have been divided more evenly. But who was he to offer an opinion? After all, he received no package at all.

The only things Jack and his buddies did get from prisoners on the other side of the wire fence were the cigarette butts flicked through to them. They would pick up the used butts, strip out any remaining tobacco, then roll the collected tobacco from several butts into a small piece of newspaper to make a homemade cigarette. The nicotine helped ease their hunger pangs.

On Sunday mornings interspersed with their work were propaganda sessions in which workers marched into the camp square for "church service" to listen to the loudspeakers tell whatever latest tale the government wanted them to believe. "Even though the Reich is experiencing some 'setbacks' right now, Hitler has a secret weapon that will soon turn things around," one speaker declared. "The Reich will triumphantly win the war, the glorious age of Germany will begin, and everyone will be free in a world of peace and prosperity." Hitler had come out with the first phase of his new weapons system when the German forces unveiled the V-1 buzz bomb and the V-2 rocket. They used the weapons on Great Britain with devastating results, and gave new impetus to their hope that the Reich would soon perfect the first atomic bomb, and Germany would be eternally victorious..

Jack listened to this information day after day and, although he didn't want to believe it, he found himself wondering if it could be correct. At the same time, he knew that something was happening to his mind that he could not control. He found himself believing what he didn't want to believe, knowing all the time that it wasn't true. When the announcements spoke of Germans being mistreated, arrested, and jailed in other countries, particularly in America, Jack discovered himself growing angry at what his birth land was supposedly doing.

"There are cases in the United States," the loudspeaker proclaimed, "in which people are so upset at the imminent success of the Reich's ventures that American soldiers are rushing into houses and mistreating German families, even butchering them!" Jack immediately feared for his mother, from whom he had had no news for nearly four years. That fear for his mother caused him to almost believe the stories, even though he recognized that they probably were false. Then he would be angry with himself for thinking they might be true. The propaganda officers repeated the stories again and again until it became easier to believe them and harder to recognize truth. Jack realized that a frightening and constant battle was raging for control of his mind. Even though he knew what they were doing to him, at times he still almost doubted his own sanity.

The factory where he spent 12 hours of each miserable day had different work sections. One day a neighboring section received new staffing, all women. Even in a weakened physical state, males, particularly at age 16, still find themselves interested in the opposite sex. As Jack passed the adjoining work section to get to his own, he couldn't help noticing a thin young blond girl. He had no idea from which country she came, but she definitely attracted his attention. Each time he passed, she was standing before her workbench, diligently doing her job as best she could, paying no attention to anyone else. She never saw him, but he kept his eyes on her as long as he could every time he passed by. The girl was attractive, but frail. He wanted to protect her, longed to get her out of there, but knew there was no possible way of doing that. Instead he just feasted his eyes on her as he went back and forth, hoping the war would end soon, and they could meet. It made his day easier to have something to look forward to each morning and evening.

Then one day when Jack walked by her work section after getting some supplies, she was gone. He could only guess that she must have collapsed at her bench, as had so many before her, and the guards had carried her out. She never came back, and although he discreetly inquired about her, he could never find out anything. Maybe they had taken her to the hospital and left her to die. Or perhaps they had simply exterminated her, deeming her no longer useful. He became even angrier at the whole idea of war. Her place was empty for a long time. Every morning when he passed by, he glanced into the neighboring work section. In his mind he could still see her standing there, an ethereal being, blond hair flowing over her shoulders. Eventually, someone else filled her bench spot, and he could no longer bear to look that way. His anger and frustration reached new levels.

Long days stretched into long weeks, then into months. The war was obviously drawing to a close, though most Germans did not want to acknowledge it. Reports seeped through that Americans had now invaded Italy and were pushing up from the south. Shortly after that, the Americans actually penetrated into Germany. Hitler was desperate. He still hoped to hold back the rest of the world long enough for German scientists to complete the atomic bomb they were working on. He had lost incredible numbers of men. His futile attempts to take Stalingrad and his later efforts to rout the Americans at the Battle of the Bulge had depleted his forces. Now the military was training young boys to defend the Fatherland. Everyone from 16 to 60 had to sign up, regardless of what important posts they must leave.

Hitler also decided to recruit political prisoners for active duty in exchange for their pardon. Now the military was willing to take anyone—even if they were maimed, mentally deficient, or handicapped. Jack called them cannon fodder. The country was so desperate for more soldiers that army recruiters came to the labor camp to recruit prisoners. Then the SS, Hitler's elite guard, showed up also. The husky SS men struck deep respect in the hearts of the inmates when they walked through the camp in their black uniforms and shiny boots, looking for the best of the volunteers.

Jack and two of his buddies got together to discuss the turn of events. "This might be a way out," Vladimir said.

"We would surely have more to eat and a warm place to stay if we volunteered," Hans agreed.

"What could we possibly lose?" Jack joined in.

Knowing they would never qualify for the SS, they volunteered for the army. The authorities readily accepted them, even though one was a Russian, one an American, and the other had been a political activist against the Reich. Leaving the detested camp, they went to a place on the other side of Nuremberg for three weeks of intensive training.

The uniforms issued them seemed to swallow up their emaciated, skeletal bodies. And they were supposed to hold back the Allies? They could hardly hold up their own pants. The new recruits paraded around the base every day, right past a German army hospital. On the verandas and in the yards sat recuperating soldiers. The wounded veterans laughed at the makeshift band of recruits marching back and forth in their ill-fitting uniforms.

Their laughter didn't matter to Jack. All he cared about was getting more to eat—and he got it. At every meal he could eat all the meat and potatoes, bread, and vegetables he wanted—reward enough for the ridicule. True, it was army food, but after near starvation, who would complain about quality? During that three-week training period, Jack shot up from 80 to 100 pounds. Compared to what he had already been through, conditions were wonderful. Now if the war would only end.

The military daily trained the recruits in how to use rifles, hand grenades, bazookas, and antitank weapons. Jack did well, and the officer in charge seemed impressed, but in the back of his mind Jack was planning a different tactic—how to escape.

At the end of three weeks the men returned to the munitions factory camp to await further orders. But now Allied planes strafed the munitions factory at all hours, carefully avoiding the prisoner-of-war sections. Often Jack, Vladimir, and Hans would have to run to the trenches to escape the bullets. As the days went by, heavier strafing produced more and more confusion. Everyone knew that the war was nearly over, and the guards had a hard time maintaining the work schedule and keeping order.

The camp had confiscated Jack's civilian clothes when he first arrived at the plant. Now the authorities gave them back. The three "volunteers" decided to wear their civilian clothes under their ill-fitting German army uniforms just in case they had an opportunity to escape. They no longer had to work at their old places because they were waiting to be assigned to the war zone, just a few miles south. All new "recruits" lived in a barrack away from the rest of the plant workers. They simply walked aimlessly around the compound waiting for orders. After a couple days, Jack and his buddies decided that it was foolish to wait any longer, hoping for a better time to escape.

"We could receive orders any day now, and we will be sent to certain death," Vladimir commented, being more familiar with military procedure.

"You know if we get caught, we will be shot. On the other hand, if we are sent to the front, we'll almost certainly die anyway," Hans reasoned.

Jack knew also that he could never raise a gun against his own American countrymen.

The three hung around the gate wearing their German army uniforms and getting better acquainted with one of the guards. Soon the German guard got so used to seeing them there, he quit paying any special attention to them. One day Hans said, "We can't wait any longer. Tomorrow night when the guard is distracted, we'll just stroll out the gate and slip around the corner of the outside wall."

"It should be fairly easy," Jack agreed, "because the guard has already allowed us to walk outside the gate a few times as long as we stayed nearby."

"After all, we *are* German soldiers now, aren't we?" Vladimir reminded them. "Fighting for the Reich just like the rest?"

The next evening, during a rare moment of trust and inattention on the guard's part, Jack and his two buddies strolled nonchalantly outside the gate at dusk. They stood there momentarily, noting that the guard was still distracted, and then slipped around the corner of the outside wall, ran across the railroad tracks, and disappeared into the nearby woods. Their hearts were in their throats. Every moment they expected guards to yell, shots to ring out, and bloodhounds to come bounding after them. The silence itself was frightening. But nothing happened. Maybe the guard thought Jack and his buddies had gone back into the compound. Whatever, the three didn't take time to wonder why they weren't being pursued. They simply pushed deep into the woods as quickly as they could.

After running for almost an hour, they stopped and listened intently. "Let's get these German army uniforms off!" Jack was already stripping off his outer shirt and pants. They smiled as they observed each other's civilian clothes, which they had worn underneath. Hiding the uniforms as best they could in the leaves and brush, they decided to head for central Germany.

All night they stumbled through the woods. Near morning Vladimir chose to head east toward the Russian front. Hans' home was in a more northerly direction, and since Jack wanted to get to Grandfather's farm, which was also in that direction, the two of them told their Russian friend goodbye with hugs and handshakes. All that day Jack and Hans pushed on without food or water. They could hear a battle in the distance and knew that the American army was much closer than they had been led to believe. The Americans seemed to be speeding across Germany without any resistance.

The second night the two young men found a road and decided to follow it. It was so pitch-dark, they could hardly see their hands held out in front of them. Suddenly out of nowhere they heard a command, "Halt!"

They froze. Out of the darkness appeared the form of a German sentry.

"Where did this guy come from?" they each thought, almost aloud.

The sentry approached with his rifle pointed at them and demanded, "Where are you going?"

Jack and his friend tried to stay calm. Since they both spoke fluent German, they answered his questions, giving as little information as possible. Whichever one felt his voice under control replied. Each one took his turn at giving names and destination. Since they were in civilian clothes and looked like displaced German children, the soldier evidently was not concerned about them. They were thankful it was dark and the sentry could not see how they were shaking.

"We are trying to reach our relatives," they stammered, and he took what they said at face value. Why he did not question them more, Jack never knew.

"Well, the road you are on is very dangerous. Allied planes are strafing everything that moves. Once it is daylight it would be most unwise to stay on this road," the soldier informed them.

"Thank you for telling us," they replied as they moved away, stumbling down the darkened road. To their amazement, they realized they were walking right through the encampment of a retreating German army unit. Soldiers slept all along the road.

As morning fully broke, they had to seek protection in a wooded area, pulling themselves over logs and fallen trees, too weak at times to take another step. The third night they began to hear gunfire in the distance. It got louder and louder as they headed for their destination. Soon they reached the top of a ridge, and there in the distance they could see Nuremberg—in flames. The Americans were shelling it.

"Looks like we won't be able to get any food there!" Hans stated simply. Now they had no choice but to circle the city, still heading toward their homes.

By morning they were in a part of Germany that was ominously still. It was a sort of no-man's-land. The Germans had retreated and the Americans were on their way. The two young men stumbled along the last few hours toward Hans' house and eventually fell into the welcoming arms of his family. After two days and three nights without food or water, the scrambled eggs, hot bread, and fresh milk seemed like a banquet from heaven. They ate ravenously. It was a meal Jack would never forget. As soon as they had finished, Jack thanked the farm family and said goodbye to his friend with hugs and handshakes. Though he desperately wanted to rest, he knew it would be best to move on.

Later, as he made his way through the woods and began getting into more familiar territory, Jack began to hear strange crackling sounds behind him like splitting trees. He quickly hid in the bushes. Approaching and gaining fast were American tanks. The Yanks were catching up with him. It was a strange sensation. Much as he hated the Nazis, he was also suspicious of the Allies. Though he wasn't sure he believed the Nazi lies planted in his mind, the brainwashing had taken its toll. All he wanted was to be left alone. He didn't trust anyone. As the

American tanks pushed in his direction, flattening everything in their way, including large trees, Jack began to panic. He still had some German equipment on him from training camp—a knife, belt, etc., all marked with the swastika. Brainwashing sessions had convinced him that Americans executed on the spot any Germans they caught. He threw his knife and belt and anything else that might identify him with the Germans into the bushes. The tanks thundered close by, but did not discover him.

Jack lay in the bushes and waited until he was sure all the tanks had passed. Then he crept to the edge of the clearing. There along the road in the valley below was an American convoy with jeeps, trucks, and personnel carriers. He would have to cross that road in order to get home, but not wanting to be seen, he sat on the hillside and simply watched what was going on below. The trucks and jeeps were loaded with GIs. One of the men in a jeep noticed him sitting there and made the American hitchhiking sign, then laughed. Since Jack was dressed in civilian clothes, the soldiers must have thought he was just a young German farm boy who didn't understand what was going on.

As Jack watched the men roll by, some of them waving to him in friendship, a sudden burst of emotion flooded his heart. In a flash, the effects of the Nazi propaganda disappeared, and all suspicions against what Americans might have done to his mother vanished. These were *his* countrymen—these were the men sent to liberate him and thousands of others imprisoned in Hitler's Reich. He had deeper roots—roots from his American childhood that embraced freedom, peace, hope for a future, and belief in a higher Power. Jack began to identify with these soldiers, his fellow countrymen. He belonged where they came from. A big smile spread across his face, and he was suddenly very proud to be an American. It was April, a month of promise, and peace flooded his heart—something he couldn't remember feeling for a long time. Jack waited until the convoy was past, then he got up, crossed the road, and headed for Grandfather's house.

As he reached the outskirts of his village, he found that its inhabitants had blocked the road with logs to keep American tanks out. He smiled to himself. Did they really think logs would stop Yankee tanks? After seeing what those tanks had done to the forest, Jack felt pity for the ignorance of the townspeople.

Walking into the village was like entering a ghost town. An eerie silence hung in the air. No one was in sight. Jack continued on to his grandparents' place and knocked on the door. Grandmother came to the door and paused there momentarily in openmouthed disbelief. Then she called Grandfather. They stood transfixed. Then Grandfather quickly pulled him in and shut the door. "The Yanks are coming! They will be here any minute, and who knows what they're going to do to us?"

Grandfather had reason for bitterness. He and Grandmother had received word about two weeks previously that Fritz would not be coming home. After surviving six years of war in France and Russia, he had been killed during the retreat through Romania just as the war was ending. While both grandparents mourned the loss of another son, Grandfather took it particularly hard. Jack could see the pain in his weathered face. He refused to talk, not only about Fritz's death, but about hardly anything, so deep was his pain. It was only after months of mourning that Grandfather would be able to speak normally again. Jack's heart ached also.

Grandmother, never idle, prepared a banquet for Jack—more scrambled eggs, homemade German brown bread, and fresh milk. In spite of the emotional upset of Fritz's death, Jack reveled in the food and being home again. Just as he finished eating, the Americans rolled into town. He and his grandparents watched from the door, marveling at how quietly the jeeps moved in. The troops got out and searched every house. When they arrived at the farm and looked it over, the American commander returned to the house and said, "I'm afraid we'll have to ask you people to go to the barn to sleep because our unit will be taking over the house for a while."

Grandmother did not take this too docilely, but she and Grandfather complied. Never once did Jack let on that he was an American. After speaking no English for more than seven years, he had actually forgotten how. He didn't want to claim to be an American and not even be able to speak the language, so he decided to wait for a more convenient time to declare himself.

For a week the soldiers occupied the house. Jeeps drove and parked all over the place. Jack smiled at Grandfather's amazement as the jeeps rolled into the farmyard and the troops climbed out. Almost immediately a loudspeaker spit out orders, the men jumped back in and started the vehicles, then wheeled their vehicles around and shot out of the yard. His grandparents had never seen anything like that in all their lives, and they marveled at what the Americans could do. No wonder they were winning the war!

At the rear of the farm the American army set up small artillery units in the freshly plowed and planted wheat field on which the family depended for food that winter. Grandfather was pretty upset. That night the artillery units shelled the nearby towns where some Germans were still trying to resist. After a week the Americans moved out, leaving only a small contingent of troops behind.

Jack, Connie, and her parents moved back into their house and returned to their regular daily routine. Actually, the Americans had behaved themselves well, disturbing no one. But some of the young German wives and unmarried girls offered themselves in exchange for chocolates, cigarettes, or nylon stockings, and the American GIs responded eagerly. It disgusted the religious-minded townspeople, especially Grandmother, to see such a thing happening in their own little town.

On May 7, 1945, Germany surrendered to the Allies. The war that was supposed to be brief was finally over. Six long and painful years of bloodshed, mistrust, and hatred had come to an end. Even the Germans felt relieved.

Chapter Eight

Home Again

Now that the war had ended and he had no chance of going to school anywhere in Germany, Jack threw himself back into the serious business of farming—at least for a while. The cities were chaotic. Little food remained, and the bombing had left buildings, roadways, bridges, and private homes virtually useless. Everything was a mass of rubble. Before the war, farmers had been the poor people, while those who lived in the cities were better off financially. Now the tables were turned. People in the cities were starving, rummaging through the garbage of the occupying forces to find food. Even those accustomed to luxury found themselves reduced to poverty. The war had been a tremendous equalizer.

But Jack and his grandparents were farmers, so they had plenty of potatoes, meat, and eggs. Compared to people in the city, they actually had it quite good. There was plenty of food for the growing, and even though it involved an incredible amount of difficult labor, Jack was glad to be doing it. He appreciated more and more the turn of fate that had brought him back to the farm and not left him dead, wounded, or eking out a meager existence in a bombed-out building of a war-ravaged city.

Jack was hungry, not only for Grandmother's good cooking, but also for freedom. He enjoyed being able to roll out of bed in the morning—even if it was at the same unearthly hour as at camp—and sit peacefully at the table to plan what needed to be done that day. It was good to work out in the fresh air with animals grazing in the field and not have a Nazi supervisor standing over him. And it was luxury to eat until his stomach no longer gnawed or growled. As weeks turned into months, he became stronger and began to put on more weight.

But in the back of his mind was the mushrooming desire to return home—home to Chicago and his mother. The isolated village had little knowledge of what was happening in the rest of the world. All they knew was that the war was over. Even news of Hitler's death had taken weeks to reach their town. A frightening rumor filtering through the country claimed that the Americans were planning to retreat and give over a large portion of conquered Germany to the Russians. Other Germans feared that the Americans and Russians would now fight it out on German soil. When American tanks carrying Russian soldiers rolled through the village, everyone was afraid that the first rumor was true—that the Americans might indeed give a large part of Germany to the Russians.

Jack's whole being revolted at the thought of being under Russian control. He would never get home to the States if that happened. He decided that if need be, he would pack up at a moment's notice and follow the Americans, walking through the woods and staying with them as far as they went. Before he could implement his plan, however, he learned to his relief that the American contingent had received orders to hold their line 10 miles north of their little village. So Jack stayed on the farm for two more months and tried to figure out how best to approach the Americans. Should he tell them that his father was Austrian and that his name should be Roess? Would that help? No, he decided, because then they might send him to Vienna, and the Russians were occupying that part of Europe. Not a good idea. How could he convince them, in spite of his German name and inability to speak English, that he really was a U.S. citizen?

One day Jack decided that, successful or not, he must go to

the American contingent in town and talk to them about his U.S. citizenship and about getting back home to the States. He wanted Grandfather to go with him as a witness of his truthfulness, but Grandfather was leery of the idea and still suspicious of Americans, so Jack went alone. After all, he was a young man of 16 now and would have to start taking responsibility for his own life.

Through a translator Jack said to the American in charge, "I am an American citizen. I was born in Chicago. Here are my papers to prove it."

The man in charge took the papers and looked them over skeptically. He discovered that Jack's last name—his mother's maiden name—was spelled two different ways on the papers. His grandparents spelled their name "Kiessling," but the American spelling that his mother used was "Kiesling" with only one "s."

"If you were born in the United States, why can't you speak English?" the man asked. "It's amazing how many 'Americans' are turning up in Germany! Frankly, I think these papers are forged."

That really upset Jack. If he had wanted to forge his papers, he would surely have done it right and not made such an obvious mistake. The American man took his papers and put him under house arrest—meaning he could not leave town—until they had thoroughly checked the documents. Jack felt his last hope of freedom had been stripped away as he walked dejectedly out of the American contingent's office and headed back to the farm.

Months dragged on, and soon autumn was in the air again. One day word came from Munich asking him to appear at the American military sub-office in Frankfurt. Jack left the next day, carrying all the food he would need, for there were no places to eat along the way. When he reached Frankfurt, the sight was sickening. The city was still one massive heap of bombed-out destruction. As far as he could see in any direction, nothing but rubble stretched endlessly. A few streets had been cleared enough to carefully navigate, so he picked his way through the city. Finally, after miles of difficult walking, Jack arrived at the designated place.

In his pocket he carried a letter he had unexpectedly received from his mother just a few days before leaving for Frankfurt. When the letter had arrived, Jack had jumped for joy. It was the first news he had had from his mother in nearly five years. She was alive! Not only that, but the letter could be proof of his citizenship, as well as his ticket to freedom. Quickly he had opened it, but because it was written in English, he could read little of it. He could make out a few phrases, but since he had finished only the second grade when he left America for Germany, he had never learned to read cursive English handwriting.

Somehow he made out enough words to know that his mother was safe and well. Jack had to take the letter to town and have someone who knew a few words of English read and translate the longhand to him. Although he had not heard English spoken for many years, he understood what the letter said. His mother had married, and Jack found out that he now had a 3-year-old sister named Marie. Katie revealed that she had tried many times to get messages to him. In one letter she had enclosed fare for a ticket home, but the letter came back "Undeliverable." She had also worked through the International Red Cross, but they had been unable to locate him. Finally, now that the war was over, she had written to Jack at her parents' home. Though she had been told that no mail would get through to anyone except military personnel, she had fervently prayed that somehow her letter would make it.

When Jack went to talk to the American officials in Frankfurt who had questioned his American citizenship, he said, "I have received a letter from my mother who is expecting me to come home to the U.S."

They laughed. "It's impossible for a letter to come through the German postal system. It's still in shambles!"

When the boy produced the letter, still in its envelope with the U.S. stamp and postmark, they couldn't believe it. "We'll have to take this to the back room and examine it," they stated.

It seemed an eternity before they returned, shaking their heads. In total amazement, the man in charge said, "The letter appears to be genuine. Looks like you're telling the truth. This proves that you didn't forge your papers." They told Jack to go back to the farm and wait for them to contact the Red Cross, who would notify his mother and then get him home.

Jack returned to the farm, ecstatic. Joyfully, he worked hard during the winter months of 1945-1946. While his grandson waited for further word from the States, Grandfather Kiessling tried to persuade him to change his mind about going back. "Jack, you are part of this family. Besides, how can we manage without you? You know if you'll stay here, the farm could one day be yours."

Fritz had been the only son interested in farming. He had been Grandfather's pride and joy, the one who would have kept the farm in the family's name. Jack's grandparents had lost two sons in the war, and their older married sons had their own careers and were not interested in the farm.

Of course, Connie still remained. She would be willing to keep the farm, but when she married, it would go under another family name. To Grandfather, this would be a blow to his pride as nothing had ever been. It would make him feel he had worked all his life for nothing. The land that had been in the family for generations would be gone. Jack was his last hope. He carried the family name from his mother, so Grandfather figured Jack could stay, marry Fritz's widow, and the farm would stay in the family. The boy knew how to work the farm, and he ran it well. He was also fond of his uncle's young wife. She was only four years older than he, and they were great friends. However, no romance existed between them, and besides, he had other plans for his life.

Grandfather's hurt was visible. Why couldn't they just fall in love? Or, maybe if they waited awhile to get married, they would naturally fall in love.

One bright spring day word came that the authorities had made arrangements for Jack to go to the U.S. He should report at once to Munich. It was a joyous day for him, though he attempted to suppress his pleasure because it was such a sad time for Grandfather and the rest of the family. He packed his few belongings that evening and the next day said goodbye to his German family at the same train station where he had said goodbye to his mother almost seven years before. A lump filled his throat from the knowledge that he was leaving his disappointed and lonely grandparents whom he had learned to love so very much.

At Munich Jack went to a camp where hundreds of people of all nationalities waited to be processed. The bunks were fairly comfortable, and the food tolerable and plentiful. To him, it was "freedom" camp, and that's all that mattered. His "work" for the day was to watch to see if the authorities had posted his name. Every day there would be a mad rush to the bulletin board when someone put up a new list of names. For weeks Jack waited, worrying that his name would never get on the list. He was sure there had been another mix-up, and they would send him back to the farm. Perhaps he should have stayed there to help Grandfather anyway. Everyone who had been waiting at the camp when he arrived seemed to have left. Jack felt sure his documents were causing trouble again.

One day as he lay on his bunk frustrated, discouraged, and about to give up and return to the farm, he struck upon an idea. *I should persuade God to get on my side, and then maybe things will work!* Although Jack had been a fairly religious person who prayed when in danger and difficulty, he feared that God might be punishing him. Staring at the wooden bunk above him, he bargained, "God, if You will help me out of this situation and get my name on that list so I can go home, I'll fast and pray for three days. I won't eat or drink a thing, I promise. And I will do it before I get back home."

Now he settled back to wait. He had done some spiritual "arm-twisting," some bargaining with God, and somehow he knew that God would now answer his prayer. In his religious training he had gotten the distinct idea that God had to be bribed, as it were, in order to get a favor. Now that he had made a bargain in which he agreed to do something for God, he knew that he would get his favor.

The next morning Jack's name appeared on the list. Along with many others he filled out documents and answered questions. Then he learned that he would go by train to Bremerhaven and there board a troop transport for the United States.

During the several hours it took for the train to reach Bremerhaven, Jack sat squeezed between lots of other people crammed on benches. He was aware that U.S. military police were guarding the passengers. Everyone had known to pack their own lunch, but Jack had decided not to take a lunch, thinking that it was a good time to do his fasting and praying, thus fulfilling the vow he had made to God two days before. Soon a GI came strolling through the train eating his lunch. His sandwich was made with white bread and stuffed with a luscious-looking filling. In those days many considered white bread an extravagant luxury, more like cake. Only the rich could afford to eat it. As the GI ate, he stopped and talked to some pretty girls. After finishing the center of his sandwich, he wadded up the crusts and tossed them out the train window. Jack couldn't believe it. What a waste! America *must* be prosperous, a land of plenty.

Before boarding the troop transport, Jack finished his last day of fasting. Then he relished food with the rest of the passengers and relaxed in the luxury of freedom, waiting only to put his feet on his native soil.

In about a week the loudspeaker bellowed, "We are now approaching New York Harbor. The Grand Lady is visible off the port side." As people rushed for the best view, Jack feared the ship would capsize. But there she was—the Statue of

Liberty—triumphantly holding her welcoming torch high above the harbor. A hush fell over the passengers—except for some indiscrete nose-blowing. As Jack took in the sight, his arms, too, broke out in goose bumps. He shivered, then realized unashamedly that his cheeks were wet. America—*his* country! He was *home!* He felt like kissing the ground. "I will *never* leave the borders of this great land again," he vowed.

As the ship steamed toward the harbor, he heard the children on board exclaiming, "Look at those skyscrapers!" Then, as their ship drew closer, he could see manicured grass and hundreds of cars speeding along the roads and across bridges. Prosperity was evident on every hand, a total contrast to the devastation of Europe.

The refugees disembarked unceremoniously and went to a hotel for the night. "The authorities are contacting relatives about your arrival," guides told them. The next morning Jack returned to the office and someone informed him, "Your mother could not get here in time, so a cousin from Brooklyn will come to pick you up today."

While Jack was sitting in the receptionist's office trying to digest this information, the telephone rang. The secretary answered, then handed the receiver to Jack. He had never spoken on a telephone in his life and had no idea how to do it. The phone stood upright on the desk with a long-stemmed receiver and a hook on the side for the earpiece. "Jah?" he proclaimed loudly into the earpiece. The girl smiled and showed him how to speak into the mouthpiece.

On the other end of the line was his cousin Nathan. "Hi, Jack, welcome back to America." Thankfully, Nathan spoke in German, since it was still spoken in his home. "I'll be there to pick you up shortly. Don't go anywhere!"

As he waited, Jack tried to remember what Nathan looked like. He had been only a child and his cousin a teenager when they had met briefly eight years ago, just before Jack and his mother had boarded the ship to Germany. Now Nathan was a grown man. Surely they would not recognize each other.

When Nathan arrived, however, it did not take long to get reacquainted and bridge the intervening years. "Your mother and her husband, Lee, with little Marie will all be here tomorrow. Their train was delayed," Nathan explained, "so we'll get to spend some time together."

They went to Nathan's home and reintroduced Jack to his aunt and uncle. "You haven't changed as much as Nathan," Jack said jovially, giving and receiving more hugs. They all seemed happy to see him and eager to hear about his experiences. His mother had sent money to buy him some new clothes. She knew he would feel odd in New York City dressed in the garb of a Bavarian farmer, and she thought he might even be in rags. After all they had heard about how terrible things were in Germany, she expected the worst. Jack did look pretty strange in his short leather breeches, knee-length stockings, and little hat. It was not exactly the attire of a 1946 American teenager.

So they went shopping. On the way Jack gazed in awe at what he saw. All kinds of displays filled the store windows. Fruit carts on the street overflowed with oranges, bananas, and pears—fruit he had not seen or tasted in years. At the department store they bought a suit for him, a pair of pants, a couple of shirts, shoes, socks, and underwear. Underwear? Jack had not worn it in years and didn't know what to do with the undershirt. "Do you wear it tail in or tail out of the undershorts?" he asked innocently. When they got home, his cousin took him into the bedroom and demonstrated how to dress properly.

Jack had learned to smoke in the labor camps, picking up cigarette butts from prisoners who received packages from the Red Cross. Nicotine calmed his hunger pangs, and smoking had become a habit. "Now that we've got your clothes, let's head for a barber and get you looking more like an American before your mother gets here," Nathan suggested. Walking down the street, Jack drew a cigarette from his pocket. A policeman stopped them, and Nathan talked with the officer in English. Later he explained, "The policeman asked why a 12-year-old was smoking since it's against the law for children to smoke. I told him that you had just come in from a German labor camp and that you are actually in your late teens." (Well, 17, but Nathan stretched it a bit.)

Finally Katie Blanco arrived. She had left behind a tearful, screaming child whom she expected to see in one short year. Now the young man she embraced, though short and thin, was mature, poised, and self-sufficient. "Oh, Jack, I am so *happy* to see you!" Now it was *her* turn to cry. "God is good," she murmured.

As for Jack, he thought his mother was the most beautiful person he had ever seen. She had not changed—not at all. Except her name. She was now married to a man of Hispanic descent—dark, handsome, and eager to meet his stepson.

But his half sister, Marie, stole his heart. Four-year-old Marie with her dark eyes, brown curly hair, and infectious laugh was at once in love with her big brother, whom she had never seen before.

Jack's stepfather's last name was Blanco, meaning *white.* Katie suggested that Jack take that name also so they could truly be one family. In those days it was confusing, if not downright embarrassing, to have a son with a different name from the mother. To make Katie happy, Jack agreed. After a few days of getting acquainted in New York, the reunited family left for Chicago.

On the train ride back Jack told his parents more about his war experiences—his escapes from death, his close calls with starvation. As he watched the green fields of America roll by, he was extremely happy to be home again. But in the back of his mind was a serious question. *What shall I do with this new life and all its wondrous opportunities?*

Chapter Nine

Starting Over

Chicago in 1946 was a busy, dirty city sprawling along Lake Michigan. Its skyscrapers rose above a maze of shops, industrial complexes, tenement houses, bars, and flimsy-looking elevated transit tracks. But to Jack it was beautiful. It was freedom. It was home. It held memories of a carefree childhood and a loving mother. Now it was even more—it was a land of beginning again.

Jack truly missed his grandfather's farm with its rustic buildings and open meadows. Sometimes he missed the quietness or the smell of newly mown hay and Grandmother's cooking. But Jack did *not* miss the long hours of walking behind the plow or of shoveling manure. What Jack wanted now was a chance to fill his mind with knowledge, something he had tried to get when he signed up for the "engineering course." At times he could not believe he had been so gullibly and naively led into a labor camp, but mostly he simply wanted to forget his skirmishes with death and near starvation.

So what if Chicago was smoky, cluttered, and sometimes unfriendly? He was home! Home, where he was loved and wanted and could walk at will through the streets without fear of the gestapo. Where he was free to get a job, go to school, or start a new life without asking permission of the state. It was strange not to have to carry identification or other papers. He could travel across town, or to another state for that matter, stay in hotels, exchange money, make purchases, cash checks, or do any number of things without police scrutiny. Also, he no longer had 14 hours of back-breaking farmwork to do every day.

All his freedom was a bit heady for Jack, so recently out of a labor camp. It was also strange to have a father around. But Jack grew to love Lee Blanco and felt grateful that he would take in a grown son and help him get his life together.

His little sister captivated the young man's heart. He spent hour after hour telling Marie about life in Germany—the farm, the tiny villages, the spiraled churches, and, of course, the animals. Little Marie had never seen cows or pigs or chickens or geese in their natural habitat. She only had looked at pictures in books and the carcasses that hung from hooks in the butcher shop. Jack remembered when he, too, had known only that life, so he tried to make existence outside the city real to her.

Jack's stepfather owned a small restaurant, in those days called a café. Nevertheless, they served food in a hurry, and it was hot and plentiful. As soon as Jack began to adjust to his new surroundings, he began to put on weight and even started to add inches to his small stature. He knew he must get a job to help with the family finances. Going to school would have to wait while he earned some money. It was only natural that Jack work for his stepfather at the café.

Though the restaurant was small, serving hamburgers, hot dogs, and similar items, it also served plate lunches and dinners. Steak, potatoes and other vegetables, as well as the usual breakfast offerings of pancakes, eggs, sausage, and toast, actually made it a full-fledged restaurant, open 24 hours a day, seven days a week. It was located in Southside Chicago, which, in those postwar years, was the tough side of town.

Jack went to work as a dishwasher at the restaurant. Electric dishwashers were still far in the future, so he spent most of his waking hours elbow-deep in dishwater. Part of his job also entailed scrubbing floors, washing windows, or whatever else needed doing. Times were hard, so Lee hired only two shifts of dishwashers, 10 hours each, then during the midnight to 4:00 a.m. hours, allowed the dishes to pile up in the sinks. When Jack arrived early in the morning, his first job always was to wash the dirty dishes and clean up things so Lee could start the day's cooking.

Since he was used to hard work on the farm and in the concentration camp, it was not too much for him. He gained 30 more pounds (50 since labor camp) and grew six inches during the first year he was home. Now, at age 18, he aspired to do things with his life that would be more interesting. Whenever he got a chance, he coaxed the cook, "Teach me all you know about cooking." Soon he became adept at it, and when the next vacancy occurred, he talked his stepfather into letting him cook.

Jack now discovered that cooking on his own was a whole new ball game. At the noon rush hour, it took not only intense physical work, but also focused attention to keep up. Instead of written orders, the two waitresses shouted orders to the cook, "One hamburger, without tomatoes or onions, one cheeseburger, loaded—hold mayo—two fries, one milk, one iced tea, and one cherry pie à la mode." It might be followed quickly by "One steak, mashed potatoes with gravy, onion rings, cole slaw, rolls and iced tea, and one pork chop, baked potato, salad, roll, and coffee with one apple pie."

Jack would call the orders back to them, remembering in which sequence they had come. Just when things seemed under control with hamburgers, steaks, chops, etc., on the grill, some joker would order pancakes. That created quite a dilemma, but somehow all the meals got out. The orders, coming as they did from two waitresses, put pressure on him to keep them straight. Once during rush hour he scalded his wrist with hot grease, but the orders kept coming, so he just tried to ignore the pain. Sometimes the next cook didn't show up, and Jack had to work a double shift. But whenever he spent 16 hours on his feet, thinking he would collapse, he would remember the guards at the camp. He recalled the cruelty with which they had enforced their orders and realized that he really had it pretty good now.

Finally, after Jack had spent months of cooking for the day shift, Lee asked him to take the night shift. It was a tough assignment, for there was a bar next door, and the late night clientele were mostly drunks, bums, or men looking for trouble. One night two sisters came into the restaurant with a man in tow. They were openly competing for his attention when a third woman joined them.

"Get your _______ _______ hands off my George!" the third woman commanded loudly as the trouble began. Presumably the man's wife, she then grabbed a bottle of beer by its long neck, slammed it against the edge of the table, and quickly jabbed the jagged, broken glass into the throat of one of the girls. "I'll teach you to come traipsing into my place trying to steal my man!" she yelled.

Screaming and bleeding, the younger woman ran outside, only to collapse on the sidewalk. Her sister and the man got her into the car and rushed her off to the hospital.

Another evening a middle-aged couple came in from the bar next door and began, first verbally and then physically, to fight with each other. The man loudly slapped his wife a couple of times, and Jack ran from behind the counter.

"Stop that!" he demanded, trying to prevent the scratching, clawing woman and slap-happy man from harming each other. When he attempted to ease between them to break it up, they both turned violently on him, cursing and shoving him, and screaming for him to mind his own business.

Finally Jack insisted, "Look, if you guys want to fight, you can't do it in here. You'll have to do it out in the street." Only his threat to call the police made them leave. After that experience, Jack vowed never again to get between a husband and wife when they were arguing.

More than once a patron of the bar next door would stagger in, drop himself partly on the counter and partly on the stool, and slur, "Gimme a hamburger (belch!) wif ev'ryding." After putting mayonnaise, the meat patty, and pickles on one side of the bun, and mustard, ketchup, lettuce, and tomato on the other, Jack would set the plate in front of his bleary-eyed customer. At that point, the inebriated man would stare at the food momentarily, roll his eyes, then fall facedown into the burger with all its trimmings.

The scene, of course, looked extremely revolting to the other patrons, so Jack would have to pick him up and clean his face—none too gently. Then Jack would drag him outside and with obvious disgust, drop him in the snow. Eventually the man would get up, shake himself, and stagger back into the bar next door.

Jack had little time to himself, but when he did have a free day, being young, energetic, and adventuresome, he naturally sought some sort of social life. As it turned out, the friends he chose belonged to a gang, and during his time off, he picked up their language and much of their gang lifestyle. Because he wanted so much to be like other Americans, it didn't take him long to absorb their habits. However, his language became so coarse that it repelled his few other friends who had higher standards.

"Jack, with your sharp mind, you really ought to at least finish high school," his mother often chided when he first returned to Chicago.

"Yeah, sure," he responded. "And how can I go to school and still work 10 hours a day?"

One day Lee Blanco came home with good news. "A customer told me today that they have a night school at the University of Chicago for people who want to finish high school."

The university was only a couple miles away, and soon Jack was taking the elevated train to the university's downtown branch after work. Later when he cooked on the graveyard shift, he went to work after getting in from evening classes. His active mind eagerly absorbed the education he had been denied for the past five years. School proved to be a double blessing, for it also took him away from his questionable friends. However, the foul language clung to him for a long time to come. Finally, a kind and helpful teacher took him aside and explained to him why Jack had so many red marks on his papers.

"This is not fit language," she explained. "Only the scum use such expressions, and those who use them are not acceptable in polite society."

Outside of his own family, it had been a long time now since he had had any contact with polite society. Of course he wanted to change the image his teacher told him he was building, so he began to make a real effort to rid himself of the habit.

Chapter Ten

Rebel

It didn't seem to Jack that he was getting anywhere very fast with his life. He did have to acknowledge, though, that the decision to go to night school was a big step in the right direction. His mind, so long focused only on survival, was thirsty for knowledge. In spite of long and sometimes odd work hours, he somehow managed to study enough to excel in class. Every week night immediately after supper, he headed for high school evening classes. He had little time for social life with this new schedule, but for now he was satisfied with exercising his long-dormant brain cells.

In part because he received credit for German as a foreign language, it took only a year and a half for Jack to finish high school. His mother had finished only grade school, so the day he received his diploma was a proud one for her.

Then one day she said with obvious concern, "Jack, you haven't been to Mass once since you came home. Don't you think you ought to give God a bit of recognition at least once in a while?"

"Oh, Mother, I just don't see any point in doing the religion thing," he responded. "I've been getting along quite well without the bother of church."

"But son, you were always a religious child. You used to enjoy going to Mass and confession. What has happened to you?"

"Mother, I've grown up now. I've learned what life is really about. Besides, I've seen so much hatred, deprivation, and death . . ." He paused in mid-sentence, then concluded forcefully, "I don't believe the church did anything during the war that I should be grateful for!"

His mother sighed. "Jack, did it ever occur to you that God may have been the very reason you came through? Perhaps He yet has a special work for you to do."

"Well," he stirred uneasily in his chair, remembering. "I *did* give God credit for saving our lives when that bomb missed us by only a few feet—in my heart, that is. Guess I never said anything out loud, though."

"Jack, Jack, you break my heart! I tried so hard to train you to love and serve God. I had hoped you might become a priest someday. You were an altar boy at Grandfather's church in the village, you know."

"Yes, but when the Nazi soldiers came and took the bells from the steeple, then said that no one should worship God anymore, it did something to me. Why would an all-powerful God allow such things to happen when people were trying to serve Him—people who are good and honest and dedicated to Him—*why?* If He were real, why would He even allow war in the first place? Why would He let all those innocent people suffer so? How could He permit torture and rape and murder and not step in to stop it? When I saw all that happening, I realized that religion is nothing but a soothing therapy for some people's souls. I don't need that kind of crutch!"

But because he loved and respected his mother, Jack consented to attend church with her when he could find the time. He had to admire her devotion. She, too, worked long, hard hours at the restaurant. Then she came home and spent more hours doing the wash, cleaning house, sewing, and working at other household chores to keep things running smoothly. She gave them a clean, happy, well-ordered home. Still, she never missed services on Sunday, and she always took time off during the week to go to confession and to burn a candle and pray for her son.

Not that he really minded sitting through the services, either. It gave him time to let his mind wander and plan what to do when he finished high school.

Every week in church he heard appeals for money. One Sunday the priest announced, "The money today will go, as it often has during the war, to help the poor people in Germany whose lives have been devastated, whose homes have been destroyed. There are many believers," the priest continued, "who are starving, living out of garbage cans. We need to give all we possibly can to help them. God will bless you for it."

The more Jack thought about what he had just heard, the more the appeal disturbed him. He had been in Germany for more than a year after the war ended and knew firsthand about the hunger and destruction there. But he could not personally recall one single time seeing his church furnish funds or food or anything else to help anyone there. The Red Cross had brought food, blankets, and medicine.

Without warning, Jack's anger at the church spewed from deep within him like an erupting volcano, totally enveloping him. Jack resented the large amounts of money solicited in church but never used to help the poor and needy. Where it actually went, he did not know, but he suddenly had no use whatsoever for the church.

Throughout the remainder of the service, he thought about the church leadership's ceremonial trappings and its vast and rich collection of paintings and other art. Then he remembered the story the nuns had told of Jesus riding to Jerusalem on a donkey. Christ had worn the simple clothes of the laboring class. The contrast between church leaders and Jesus Christ thundered a message to Jack. He could see very little being done for the poor and needy in Southside Chicago, let alone in Germany. Never would he be so gullible again. "This will be my last encounter with religion!" he determined as he left church that day.

When he discussed his thoughts later with his mother, she

was tearful. But he only grew more agitated and adamant. "Why doesn't the church sell some of those treasures piled up in the Vatican and feed the poor? Why do poor people like us have to try to feed the needy? Fifty thousand dollars the priest wants from this congregation! We're all hardworking people, barely keeping body and soul together, and the Pope and bishops live in splendor! It doesn't make sense, Mother!"

After a brief pause, Jack became even more intense in his denunciation of the church. "It doesn't even let you decide how much money you can give! It's outrageous! To think that they actually send you a bill each month for what they decide is your share. It's grand larceny, I tell you! You don't owe anything to that church." He paced and gestured as he continued. "Then if you don't pay on time, you get notices and even veiled threats as to what will happen to you and your family—at least in the afterlife, if not in this one—unless you pay your stipulated part. Personally, I find it so disgusting, I don't want any more to do with it!"

Finally he sank into a chair, exhausted from his fiery speech. His mother studied him with pitying eyes and a look of sadness that silently asked, "Where did I go wrong in my training?"

Things were not going well in Europe, and with the Russians cutting off supplies to West Berlin, the United States put the Berlin airlift into action. America needed more young men in the military, so it reactivated the draft. As a result, Jack immediately decided that college would be a worthwhile pursuit for him. After graduating from high school evening classes, he planned to enroll at the University of Chicago. His mother was proud. Now her son would be a college man.

Living near the university exposed him to extreme rationalism and even more religious skepticism, including criticism of the Bible. Jack tormented his mother with theological questions whenever they discussed anything. "Mother, you know it's impossible for a virgin to have a baby! That's no different from some of those pagan religions who claim their gods have fallen from the sky. All that religion stuff is pure bosh! There is no God, no Creator, no guiding Spirit. We just live our lives the best we can and get out of it what we can. After death, there is nothing. I say have fun while you can. It's all you're going to get!"

Still interested in becoming an aeronautical engineer, he wanted to fly. Such a career surely would make him a wealthy man. He'd had enough farming. Enough dish washing. Enough cooking.

By now he had started drinking—only socially and occasionally, but it seemed to be expected more and more often with his associates. He had determined he would never be an ordinary drunk—he had seen enough of that at the restaurant. Instead, he would drink only enough to get the feeling of well-being. However, one night at a rowdy party with some university friends he knew he had gone beyond that point.

"Come on, Jack, be a man! We're going out to the parking lot. Joe has some really good hard liquor in his car."

Jack had observed that when a person already inebriated was exposed to cold air, the effects of his drinking became much more pronounced. He would virtually lose all control of his thoughts and actions. While Jack was dimly aware that he had already had too much, in the cold air of that bitter winter night he could not seem to stop. Accepting the challenge to have some hard liquor also, he and his friends sat in the car and drank for quite a while. Then they all decided to go back inside the house. By now Jack was extremely drunk and could no longer control himself at all. Strangely enough, he knew it, and though he wanted desperately to regain command of himself, he simply could not. Neither his mind, his body, nor his tongue would respond to his wishes.

Jack made a ridiculous fool of himself in front of his friends and many strangers. Though he had always shown great respect for women, he now found himself doing vulgar things in their presence, using coarse and suggestive language. With everyone laughing and egging him on, he became the clown of the evening. Although he felt embarrassed, he seemed unable to stop. Finally, when he had thoroughly exhausted himself, someone took pity on him and offered to drive him home. Too drunk even to climb into the car, Jack found himself dumped unceremoniously on the floor of the back seat, where he proceeded to vomit all over the car, his topcoat, and his suit.

Once home, Jack was vaguely aware of his mother's quiet voice as she dragged him to bed and removed his clothing. Sobbing her heart out as she cleaned him up, Katie then gently covered him and left him to sleep it off.

Obviously, he did not go to work that day. The house was empty, and as he recovered from his hangover, he well remembered what an absolute fool he had made of himself. His head ached miserably. As rationality returned and he had time to think, he realized that he was now regaining control of his body again. He vowed that never again would he touch hard liquor. From now on, it would be only light wine or an occasional mug of beer.

Before his first semester at college even began, however, the draft board discovered that Jack had never served in the U.S. Army. The officials notified him to sign up for the draft now that he was 19. It didn't matter that he had been forced to serve briefly in the German army or that he had spent years in a labor camp. He was in the United States, and he must fulfill his duty to his country in the same way as any other young American.

A brochure made Jack first consider joining the Coast Guard and applying for Officer's Training School, which he figured would at least keep him close to U.S. shores. But he was not really excited about any kind of military service unless it involved flying. He had wanted to become an aeronautical engineer in Germany and had gotten sidetracked. Now he decided to try again. One thing for sure, he was not going to be a foot soldier if he could help it.

Jack's decision disappointed his mother and Lee Blanco. If he joined the U.S. Army, he would be out in 18 months. But if he signed up with the Air Force, he would be gone from three to five years. By that time—who knew?—maybe there would be another war, and he would wind up overseas somewhere again.

It also frustrated his parents to learn that he had no intention of staying in the restaurant business. They had hoped that he would someday take it over. While it would not make him rich, there would be an honest living in it. Jack was adamant, however, about that.

"Why in the world," his mother asked, "would you put yourself into such a dangerous situation as serving in the Air Force when you could soon be back, nice and safe right here in Chicago? You could get married, settle down in a nice apartment, and run the restaurant."

Her husband added, "Jack, you always wanted me to turn this into a fast-food drive-in chain. You said it was the wave of the future. That doesn't appeal to me at all, but you could do it. You could have it just the way you want it."

"No, Lee. I think it would make you a lot of money, and if I were to take it over, that's just what I'd do. But I am not interested in restaurant work as a career. I want to fly. I'm too restless to settle down in one place for the rest of my life."

First, he had disappointed his grandparents by not taking over the family farm in Germany and keeping it going for another generation. Now he was disappointing his mother. Well, a fellow had to live his own life, didn't he?

So in July 1949, having just turned 20, Jack said goodbye to his family and set out in search of new adventures in the U.S. Air Force. Where it would eventually lead him could not have surprised him more.

CHAPTER ELEVEN

The Search

San Antonio was hot, dusty, and windy. Basic training in the Air Force was much the same as any other branch of service—long hours of intense physical workouts, drill practice, cleaning barracks, inspections, standing at attention, learning to salute properly, running obstacle courses, and performing KP duty. Each night the recruits fell into their bunks totally exhausted, with sore muscles, blistered feet, and thin tempers. Jack was probably better conditioned to such rigors than some, but it was wearing on everyone.

Fights often erupted in the barracks, even though strictly forbidden. In fact, such fights often furnished the evening entertainment. Jack loved to be in the middle of everything and was quick to explode. One night a disgruntled soldier shoved Jack into his bunk. "Out of my way, you shrimp!" the husky recruit sputtered as he strode darkly toward his own bed. Jack jumped up and retorted with a glancing right blow to the young airman's face, forgetting the other soldier's reputation as an experienced fighter. Before he knew what had happened, Jack found himself lying on the barracks floor with a deep gash across the bridge of his nose from his dog tags. His nose bled profusely and became swollen and painful.

He was afraid to have the gash treated, however, for fear of severe discipline. Besides, he didn't think his nose was really broken. But he began having trouble breathing, and once the

Air Force transferred him to another camp, he went to the medical clinic there.

"Well, Private, your nose has been broken," the doctor confirmed. "It appears to be knitting back in such a way as to cause breathing problems."

Jack received no other treatment. However, he did conclude after the experience that he was neither big enough nor trained enough to match skills with an experienced fighter, and he calmed down considerably.

Three months after finishing basic training, he went to Cheyenne, Wyoming, to specialize in radio, teletype, and ground communications. He enjoyed his work, but certain observations about the Air Force and life in general began to seriously trouble him. It bothered him that he observed so little honor, valor, and loyalty. No matter where he looked, time after time he found himself extremely disappointed in his fellow human beings. It bothered him that everyone appeared to look out only for himself. No one seemed to care if getting to the top caused another person to suffer. Integrity, faithfulness, a person's word—all meant nothing. A promise was made to be broken—unless, of course, it was convenient or self-serving.

He searched repeatedly for role models, especially among the officers, and found none that satisfied him. He expected leaders to be exemplary, but it seemed that the war had wiped out all heroes and brought an end to high standards and ideals. He knew *he* was no saint, liking a good time as well as the next fellow. Partying, movies, drinking, novels, smoking, and profanity were fundamental in his life. But somehow, he expected more of his leaders. Human existence seemed so shallow and empty, and his disappointment in others was keen. Surely there was more to life than this! Jack longed to meet someone different—someone with a decent conscience. He would admire and emulate a person like that, if he could find one. If only he could discover a friend he could trust, someone in whom he could confide.

Perhaps the fact that Jack had been raised without a father had something to do with his insatiable desire for a strong role model. While he had certainly admired his uncles and his grandfather, even they didn't take the place of the father he had needed for companionship, love, and acceptance. His stepfather was a fine man also, but Jack still felt a serious lack in his personal life. Wasn't there someone somewhere who could meet his ideal of a noble character and strong morals?

One day, alone in the barracks, he lay on his bunk looking at the ceiling, hands clasped behind his head, thinking about his need for a trusted friend. "Where would I find such a person?" he asked himself. "Where can I find a man of loyalty, integrity, honesty, and trustworthiness?"

Then, as if an audible voice had spoken, the answer came in profound simplicity: Jesus Christ.

Jack sat bolt upright on his bunk. That wasn't at all what he had been looking for. No, not at all. It seemed *too* simplistic. But somehow he realized that it *was* the answer to his questions. With embarrassment, he recalled his earlier declaration that Christianity was a fraud. Now he realized that he himself had been duped. Of *course*—only one Person could possibly fill an individual's deepest needs. God had designed human beings that way.

"Jesus *is* the answer!" Jack acknowledged in childlike wonder.

As he lay back down on his pillow, somewhat awestruck, he realized that the Holy Spirit had spoken, perhaps directly, to his very soul. "If only I could have lived back when Jesus did, I would have followed Him without question!" Memories of his early training began to come back to him. He remembered certain Bible stories, the Catholic sisters saying at school that Christ is always with us, even today. The thought expanded inside his head. *He* is *here*—today! *I can follow Him* now! Then, barely audibly, Jack said, "I *will* follow Him. He *is* the perfect one. I'll start to follow Him right *now!"*

When the full realization swept over Jack that God personally cared about him, it caused a 180-degree turn in his reasoning. God did not—would not—have to be bargained with first. He seemed to have reached down, taken Jack by the shoulder, and turned him gently in the exact opposite direction from the way he had been going. From that moment the focus of his life became How can I follow Jesus? Every act, every decision, must now be made in light of What would Jesus do?

He still wanted nothing to do with churches or organized religion. All he desired was to follow this Man who he knew would somehow change his life and make him a better person. More than anything, he wanted to be like Jesus—honest, reliable, loyal, trustworthy, and dependable, but he realized he was a long way from that lofty goal.

Jack knew he had a lot of sins to confess before he could really call himself a follower of Jesus, but he didn't know quite how to go about it. In spite of his discomfort with the Catholic Church, he decided that he must get his confession of his sins over with, so he went to the priest on the base. It was the only thing he knew to do. As he feared, however, his visit to the confessional booth did nothing at all to soothe his soul.

Not knowing anyone else he could consult, Jack knew he must figure out alone how to follow Jesus. Though he must do it himself, he realized he was not totally alone. Every morning he lay in his bunk a few extra moments with his eyes shut. "Jesus," he prayed, "would You walk by my side today? I don't know how to ask, but I know I need You to guide me in all I do. Please help me."

After a few days he began to think that maybe he could confide in Jesus directly, and talk to Him as a friend. Would that be too audacious? Jack then got more personal with his prayers. "Jesus, maybe I shouldn't be just coming out and asking You myself, but I know You came to this world to save people. I haven't been a very good person, so I really need You—probably more than anyone. Please forgive me for . . ." Jack then specified a number of his failings.

He had full confidence that his new Friend could and would help him, even without going through an earthly mediator. Once he realized that this *was* walking with Jesus, he knew that his sins *were* forgiven. His heavy burden of guilt vanished.

At the same time, he somehow sensed that the real power of the gospel would manifest itself in the change it brought to his life. He had to know, to experience, that God's grace could and would change his life here and now. In a sense, he put God on trial.

"God, can You change even me? Can I become the person I ought to be, right here? If that really could happen, then I would know that Your grace is real."

Daily he tried to imagine what it would be like to have Jesus literally walking beside him. Almost immediately he knew that Jesus would never pull out a pack of cigarettes and offer him a smoke. So he decided to get rid of his cigarettes. Just that morning he had bought a couple of cartons of Philip Morris and put them in his footlocker. That night he took them out and offered them to one of his buddies.

"Why are you doing this?" Frank asked suspiciously.

"I'm quitting," Jack said, pressing the cartons upon him.

"Oh, yeah? I've heard that before. In a few days you'll be asking me to give them back to you."

"No, Frank, I won't," Jack answered with assurance. "I'll *never* smoke again."

"OK, I'll take them—if you promise never to ask for them back."

"I promise," Jack pledged, and the young man gleefully accepted the cartons and took them to his own locker.

A couple years later Jack met Frank as he was returning from the Far East. "Hey, Jack, are you wanting those cigarettes back?" the former buddy joshed.

Jack smiled. "No, Frank. I haven't smoked since that day, and I don't ever intend to again."

It seemed that *Something* kept bringing certain of Jack's bad habits to his mind. "If Jesus were present," he mused, "I would never use profanity." Jack thought about that for quite a while. He knew that when women were present, he could always manage to curtail his speech and use only respectful and courteous words. If he could do it for women, why couldn't he do it for Jesus? But it was harder than he thought, and he caught himself many times, but it helped to remember that Jesus was right beside him, hearing every word.

The awareness of his yen for an occasional drink began to trouble him. Since that night at the party when he had so thoroughly disgraced himself, he had never again drunk hard liquor. But he still enjoyed a beer now and then, and occasionally, a glass of wine. At first, he tried to reason away the wine. "Lord, I'm almost certain the Bible says that Jesus drank wine," he tried to bargain. But somehow he didn't think Jesus would take anything that would cloud His mind even a little bit. So he gave up all alcoholic drinks. The Holy Spirit was accomplishing quite a work, for Jack had never even held a Bible in his entire life. His battle against sin and self centered entirely around "What would Jesus do?"

Now he reluctantly decided to search for a church. The only one he knew about and felt comfortable with was the Catholic Church. But after his confession to the priest in which he experienced no sense of forgiveness or satisfaction, he decided to do some research. He went to the base library and searched for answers to some of his questions.

One day, looking through the shelves, he came across a book with a green cover and the word *Bible* on it. Not knowing what a Bible really looked like, he said to no one in particular, "This must be a Bible!" Removing it from the shelf, he took it over to one of the reading tables. The book fell open to a picture of Jesus standing with outstretched arms. At His feet sat all kinds of people, some with crutches, some blind. Old people, young people. Underneath the picture was written, "Come unto Me, all ye who labor and are heavy laden, and I will give you rest."

Instantly, Jack saw in his mind's eye the Communion table in the little village church in Germany. Those same words had been carved on it. Across his mind flashed memories of all the providential things—yes, even miraculous things—that God had done for him already in his short life.

Remorse filled him. Tears began flowing down his cheeks and he longed to sit at the feet of Jesus, as did those in the picture, and tell Him how sorry he was for being such a wretched sinner and requiring such a sacrifice from God Himself. Tears splashed on the book. Quickly he wiped them away, hoping that no one had seen him crying. Then he returned the book to the shelf and somberly walked out. His private confession, known only to his Father, sealed further Jack's commitment to God.

That book at the library was like a magnet. Every spare moment he returned to read it. One of the first things he discovered was that the dead rest in the grave until Jesus comes (1 Thess. 4:13-18; Eccl. 9:4, 5). It did not make much sense to think that the dead went to heaven or hell, only to go back to the grave so they could then be returned to where they had already been. According to the book, dead people just slept until the coming of Jesus, then the final judgment took place.

The book he had discovered was in the form of questions and answers, and Jack fell in love with it. He noticed that the library had two copies, so he decided to just take one so he could have it with him all the time. It meant so much to him that he did not feel guilty of stealing such a gold mine of comfort and knowledge. He would simply check it out and conveniently forget to return it.

The green-bound "Bible" meant a lot to Jack. Studying it in the library had brought him closer to the Lord. It had helped to convert him and helped him know how to confess his sins. He felt acceptance because of the book. No longer was he following a mere human hero. The book brought his Saviour close to him.

Soon it was time to be transferred out. His conscience began to bother him, telling him he should do something about the book. Living so much closer to Jesus had helped him realize that to keep it would not be right. The day before he was to leave, he went to the librarian, confessed what he had done, returned the book, and paid his fine. She didn't seem upset about it at all. (Years later he was to learn that his "Bible" was in reality an early edition of the book *Bible Readings for the Home Circle.* Someone had cut out the sections about the Sabbath, had the book rebound, and labeled it simply "Bible." It would be some time yet before he discovered that Bibles do not come in question-and-answer form.)

Jack was going to be sent to the Far East. He had asked to go to Germany so he could see his grandparents again, but as is usually the case, the military decided to send him elsewhere. He had a 30-day furlough before being shipped out, so he returned to Chicago for a long visit with his parents and little sister.

Having quite a bit of time on his hands while his parents were at work, he decided that somehow he must find another Bible. He went to all the bookstores he could locate.

"Oh, yes, we have every kind of Bible that's published. Would you prefer King James or the Douay Version?"

What does King James have to do with the Bible? he wondered. Douay meant nothing to him, either. "What I'm looking for," he explained, "is one with questions and answers."

No one knew what he was talking about, and everyone he asked assured him that no such version existed. But Jack knew better and continued his search. For four weeks he looked in every Chicago bookstore, the booksellers insisting there was no such thing, and Jack replying that he had read one in a library. Finally, at the very last store on his list, someone told him about a bookstore on the north side of Chicago owned by an old man who had every kind of book printed. If such a book really existed, he would surely have it.

Time was running out. Jack had only two days left, so he hurried to the elevated train track and rode to the north end of town. The address was difficult to locate, and he had to walk some distance. When he finally reached the correct address, a sign on the door said "Closed for Lunch. Back at 1:00."

So Jack went across the street, had a cup of coffee, and waited. At 1:00 p.m. he returned, but the store was still closed. He waited until 1:15. Then 1:30. At 1:45 he was about to give up and head for home when an old man with a cane came hobbling down the walk. Sure enough, it was the owner. He apologized for being so late.

"Now what is it you are looking for, young fellow?" the old man asked, unlocking the door.

"I'm looking for a Bible in question-and-answer form. I know there is one, for I read one at the base library, but I can't find another like it."

"Hmmmm," the old man thought for a long moment. "Maybe I can help you. Come with me."

Jack followed him to a dark and dingy back room where dusty old books reached all the way to the ceiling. The old man got a ladder and a feather duster and climbed to the top shelf. Shortly he dusted a book off and brought it down.

At first glance it did not look like the same book. A lot thicker, it was the same green but had a picture embossed on it. Nor did it say "Bible" on the cover, but Jack opened it and began looking through it. Sure enough, it was in question-and-answer form, so he turned to the section entitled "State of the Dead" and was overjoyed to find that it was identical to the one he had read in the Cheyenne library.

"Eureka!" he shouted. "I've found it!"

The old man smiled indulgently.

"How much do you want for it?" Jack then asked eagerly, willing to pay any price.

"Two dollars will do," the old man said, and led the way at a slow hobble back to the cash register. Jack joyfully paid for it and set out for home. Carefully he packed his newfound treasure into his duffel bag. Now he was ready to go overseas.

CHAPTER TWELVE

Headaches

Jack, it's so good to hear you talk without using curse words all the time," Katie Blanco whispered as she hugged her son goodbye. "I hope you'll keep it up once this threat of war is over!"

"Well, I'm trying," he answered hopefully, "and God seems to be on my side."

"We love you, dear. Do be careful, and we'll be praying that you don't have to go to Korea." She and Lee were uneasy about his future.

"Do you *have* to go?" 8-year-old Marie wailed as Jack turned to leave.

"Chin up, kiddo. I'll be back before you know it!" he promised, tugging her pigtail. Then he was gone.

Leaving Chicago, he returned to Cheyenne, only to be whisked to San Francisco, then to Japan—first Tokyo and then Yokohama. After a few days of shore leave, a large contingent of troops, including Jack, shipped out for Guam.

That tiny island was hot and very humid—30 miles long and four to 10 miles across. Mosquitoes buzzed everywhere. If his arms rested against his mosquito netting during the night, they would be peppered with red dots by morning. Toads, which the Japanese had brought in to help control the mosquito problem, proliferated unmercifully, perhaps because of their good mosquito diet, but it didn't seem to decrease the mosquito population!

Humpty-dumpty before the fall

Katie (seated) with a couple of her coworkers

Aunt Elke's balcony, similar to the one Jack fell from

A slender Jack after the sitter put him on a "diet"—taken just after moving in with Aunt Elke

First day of school

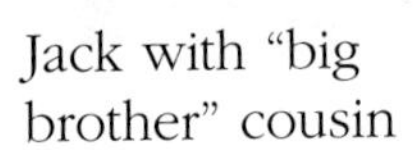

Jack with "big brother" cousin

Second grade, shortly before leaving the States (check the impish look, third from left on front row)

With Mother and "big sister" cousin

Joseph with the gentle-nosed oxen

The Keisling family (front left to right: Grandfather, Connie, Mother, Grandmother; rear left to right: Joseph, Fritz, unnamed uncle, Uncle Jack, unnamed uncle)

Altar boy in Germany

With Grandfather in a rare moment of inactivity

Fritz and his bride on their wedding day

Shortly before Pearl Harbor brought the U.S. into the war

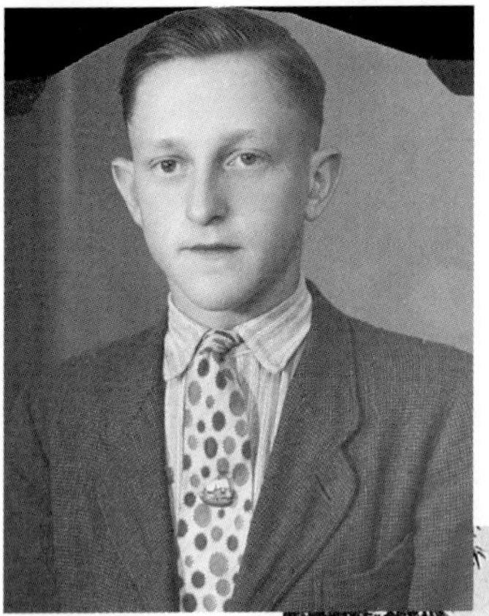

After the war, shortly before returning to the U.S.

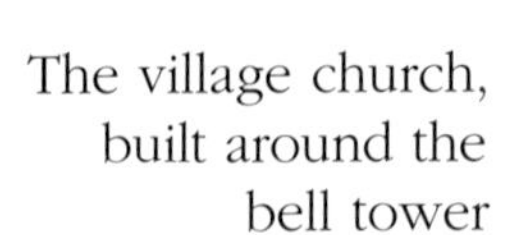

The village church, built around the bell tower

Grandmother and Grandfather in rare "dress-up" moment

With Mother and Marie

With Lee and Mother shortly after returning to Chicago

The blue lagoon where Jack's and Carl's baptism took place

Wedding day

On Guam

Jack leading the song service at a New Jersey evangelistic meeting

Pastor and Mrs. Osgood

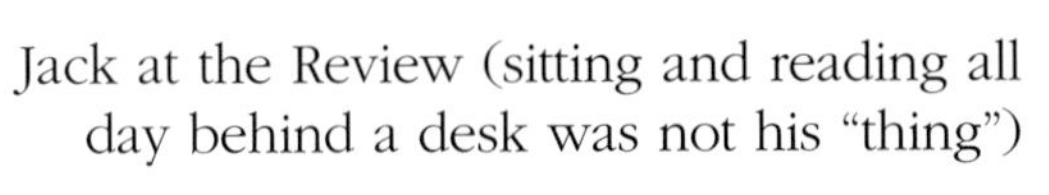

Jack at the Review (sitting and reading all day behind a desk was not his "thing")

Graduation from the Seminary with proud Mother Katie and Lee, Cheryl Ann, and Stephen

Stephen (2) and Cheryl Ann (5)

Princeton graduation, June 1965

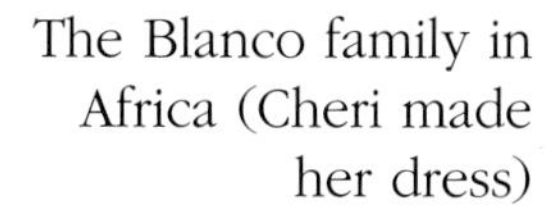

The Blanco family in Africa (Cheri made her dress)

Jack and some of his students (and Steve and Cheri) with a small congregation they helped establish a few miles from Solusi

Reunited with Carl (Pinterich) in Texas (1980)

The Philippine Union College gym (across from the Blanco home) after a hurricane

Jack Blanco in the nineties

"Listen to this Guam-eze lullaby!" the jeep driver yelled back through the wind as they rode along. Jack could hear a sickening *Squish, squish, squish* as one after another toad met its untimely end.

"Where do you go to *do* something?" Jack questioned after about a week.

"Hey, man, you're imprisoned in paradise. Get real! There's no way to get off this island—no leaves, no furloughs, and no place to go." Before long Jack developed a serious case of what the servicemen called "Rock Fever."

However, he found he could escape the reality of the island through his love of reading. Strangely, now that he owned the book he had sought so fervently, he never read it. Instead, he disappeared into a fantasyland of detective stories and romantic novels. His "Bible" had become merely a symbol, a sacred icon. Others had medals of saints or golden crosses around their necks. He had his "Bible" safe in his locker, even though he never found time to read it.

"Now that I've quit all that wild behavior, I need something to occupy my mind," he reasoned as he picked up a new novel. "Besides, an idle mind is the devil's workshop." So he read avidly.

He felt he was now really behaving himself. After all, hadn't he totally given up drinking and partying? He thought—based on the idea that he was not doing anything bad—that he was being good. It didn't occur to him how that reasoning caused him to focus his attention on himself and not on his Saviour.

"Don't you ever get tired of those books?" his buddy Don questioned one evening. "Come go to the movie with us. It's free, and it sure beats reading dumb books all the time."

Jack agreed, and decided it was easier than reading. In fact, he frequented the base movie house so often that he saw most movies several times. When a friend went with him, Jack delighted in reciting everything that was about to happen, disgusting his partner. Ultimately, he could no longer talk anyone into accompanying him to the movies.

By then, he had concluded that all novels and movies were basically the same—and boringly repetitive. "I'm not thinking very much about Jesus anymore at all!" it suddenly dawned on him one day. Reflecting on this, he couldn't imagine Jesus wanting him to immerse himself in the kind of reading and viewing he had been engaging in when there was so much of eternal value to concentrate on. So he quit reading paperbacks and almost stopped attending the movies.

Then his friend Don tried to get him to go one more time. "There's a new movie playing tonight that you might really enjoy," he told Jack. "It's based on the Bible."

"What's the name of it?"

"David and Bathsheba."

"Yeah, that might be a good one to see."

It was interesting, but it really didn't seem to help him spiritually. The theme was shallow, the plot emphasized only the tawdry, and it left out almost any mention of spiritual implications. "No more movies for me, not even Bible movies," Jack told himself. But he still ignored his *Bible Readings* volume.

The men worked block shifts of eight hours on, then had eight hours off before working another eight hours. After three such shifts in two days, he had the next 24 hours off, only to repeat the previous schedule at the end of the day off. It was awkward and confusing to the body clock. Shortly after the fight in Texas when his nose had been smashed against his dog tags, Jack began having migraine headaches. Now, combined with his crazy schedule, the migraines became more and more severe. The pain started in the back of his head and moved forward. Nausea would then set in, and he would start vomiting every hour, then every half hour, eventually every 15 minutes—the pattern extending over several hours. Finally, it began to taper off to every half hour, then every hour before ultimately subsiding. The whole ordeal often lasted 24 to 36 hours, and when it was over, he would be totally drained. Medical science in those days had no medication to stop migraines. The doctors examined him and worked some more on his nose, but still the headaches didn't stop. They finally decided that if his headaches didn't cease, they would have to send him home. Actually, he wouldn't have minded that, but the headaches were even worse a problem than having to stay on Guam, so he began to self-diagnose himself.

He noticed that when he drank strong black coffee (which he often did to stay awake at such odd hours), he ended up with a headache, sometimes mild, but often severe. Jack quit drinking coffee, and the headaches subsided. However, they soon returned, and this time he connected the headaches with eating pork chops, a food he dearly loved. So he gave up pork, and again the headaches stopped. Next went caffeinated soft drinks. The same thing happened. It seemed a lot to give up to feel good, but in the end he felt it was more than worth it.

During all his experimentation, Jack ended up in the hospital again with a bad migraine attack. After a day or two the headaches faded but left him extremely weak. The doctor decided to keep him an extra day so he could rest up. A Christian magazine caught his attention, but it had a picture of Christ on the front, and with all the cynicism and profanity on every hand at the base, he really wasn't ready for anyone to know that he had an interest in spiritual things. Carefully folding the cover to hide Jesus' picture, he started to read. The first words he read were "I am not ashamed of the gospel of Christ because it is the power of God unto salvation."

The gentle rebuke shook him. *How could I deny the very Man I'm trying to follow, the One I admire, the One with all the perfect qualities? How could I do that to Him?* Immediately, Jack unfolded the magazine and unashamedly read it with the cover plainly in view.

Some evangelical Christians in the hospital soon engaged him in a religious discussion, asking if he was saved by grace.

"Oh, you're a Catholic," they said when they learned his background. "You believe you're saved by works. That's not according to the Bible."

Jack didn't understand what they were talking about. Mistaking his confusion for lack of conviction, they handed him a Bible. "Look up Ephesians 2:8 and 9," one of them said. "Can you find it?"

Not wanting to be embarrassed, and thinking of his own Bible in question-and-answer form, he was sure he could find that text, so he answered, "Yes, I'll find it." He took their Bible and opened it confidently. In all his life, he had never been so confused trying to find something in a book. It had different names for each of the sections, plus chapters, columns, and verses, with numbers all over the place.

Finally, he gave up and admitted sheepishly, "I don't guess I can find it." The other GIs found the text and read it aloud to him: " 'For by grace are ye saved through faith; and that not of yourselves: it is the gift of God: not of works, lest any man should boast.' " They read more and continued to speak of the difference between faith and works.

"Well, fellows, I don't even understand what you're talking about. In my simple mind, what you believe, you do, and what you do, you believe. How can a person desire virtue and not at least strive to be virtuous himself?" Jack didn't indulge himself in worry about the theological points they were trying to make. However, he did learn from the experience what a Bible is, so he went to the library to get better acquainted with a real Bible.

Genesis . . . Exodus . . . Leviticus . . . Spiritually hungry, Jack wanted to read and absorb every page methodically. He found his study absolutely fascinating, even though it took many long hours in the base library. Somehow it didn't occur to him to go to the chaplain's office and request a Bible of his own.

His friends Mervyn, George, and Don returned to the base one day sporting tattoos they had gotten in town. "Just look at the details of this flagship!" George said proudly, flexing his biceps.

"Wow! That is beautiful. How much does it cost?"

"It's really cheap here," Don said. "Much less than back in Chicago."

"Hmmm. I might like to get one for my mother's sake," Jack told them. He loved her and figured a tattoo would be a way to honor her. But about that time he discovered a text in Leviticus that forbids tattoos (Lev. 19:28).

"I never knew God said anything about that!" he uttered aloud after reading it.

"Shhhh!" someone in a nearby carrel hissed.

It didn't take long to figure out that he should put God's word even before doing something he felt would honor his mother, a choice that would help in a bigger decision he must later make.

The Holy Spirit was relentless in bringing personal habits and practices to mind that Jack needed to change. Even the *Reader's Digest*, through an article about J. C. Penney, was instrumental in making him aware of a biblical principle. The story told how Mr. Penney faithfully gave 10 percent of his earnings to the Lord throughout his life, and the Lord had remarkably blessed him in many ways.

"What a novel idea!" Jack exclaimed, though he had no thought of getting rich. He began giving 10 percent of his pay to the Catholic Church, feeling grateful for this small way to tangibly express appreciation for what God had done for him.

What else would God reveal to Jack? Well, if there really was more, Jack was ready to accept it—*anything*, as long as it came from God's Holy Book.

CHAPTER THIRTEEN

Carl

Word got out that Jack had become religious, and another young airman who was also searching for spiritual truth stopped him one day. "I understand that you're interested in religious things," Carl said.

"I guess you could say that," Jack answered with a smile.

"Well, I have a book on the life of Christ you might be interested in, called *The Desire of Ages*. It came from the Bible correspondence school from which I'm taking lessons."

"Why, yes, that sounds interesting. I'd like to read it."

The two went to Carl's barrack, and as he pulled out the book, Carl volunteered, "By the way, I understand this book was written by a woman who had only three grades of education. But it's quite good."

"When do you want it back?"

"No hurry. Just let me know what you think of it."

Jack took the book back to his own barrack, and since he was off that night and the rest of the guys were out drinking, he pulled the mosquito netting around the bunk, propped up on the pillow, and began to read. Soon he found himself thoroughly engrossed in it. Several chapters later, he put the book down and said to himself in utter amazement, "This woman was inspired!" It was a conviction that stuck with him for the rest of his life.

He read long into the night, before sleep finally overtook

him. Jack simply could not get out of his mind its themes of God's amazing grace and the awesome sacrifice that Jesus had made on *his* behalf. When he returned the book a couple of days later, Carl asked, "Well, how did you like it?"

"I've never read anything like that book!" Jack enthusiastically responded. "The author was definitely inspired!"

Carl smiled. Having learned much from the Bible correspondence school in which he was enrolled, he was brimming with information he felt compelled to share. "Did you know you're going to church on the wrong day?" he asked.

"What do you mean?" Jack countered defensively.

"Well, the Bible says that the *seventh* day is the Sabbath, not the first day."

"How do you know which is the seventh day?"

"Look at the calendar and count." Carl pointed to the wall.

Jack turned around and spotted Carl's calendar. Quickly he counted. Sure enough, the seventh day *was* Saturday. (Later he learned that such evidence could be considered superficial, but to his receptive, searching mind, it was enough.)

"You're right! But how did you know to keep the seventh day?"

"From the Bible."

"Show me."

Carl took his Bible, opened it to the Ten Commandments, and read them all aloud.

"Which Bible are you reading from?" Jack asked suspiciously.

"King James."

"Isn't that a Protestant Bible?"

"Yes."

"Well, I'm not going to believe a Protestant Bible. I'll have to get a Catholic Bible and see what it says." Even though Jack had read the story of the Ten Commandments earlier on his own, he had not caught the significance of the seventh day that Carl had now pointed out.

A couple of days later Jack went to see the Catholic chaplain to buy a Bible. The chaplain was out, and his assistant said, "I'm sorry, but I can't let you have a Bible. The chaplain likes to hand them out himself so he can explain to people how to understand it better. He would be angry if I let you have one without that instruction."

"Look," Jack answered impatiently, "I can go to the library and get one to read any time I want, so what's the difference?"

The assistant finally agreed—if Jack would promise not to tell anyone who had sold it to him. "That will be $2," he said as he reluctantly handed Jack a paperback edition of the Douay Version.

Jack thanked him and winked. "I don't need a receipt. You can put the money into the offering, and no one has to know."

When he got back to the barrack, Jack turned to the Ten Commandments and read how the Lord had given them—how He had actually written them with His own finger. To Jack's amazement and horror, they seemed to read exactly like the Protestant King James Version that Carl had used. Jack was incredulous. How could his own church, to which he had now returned, teach the commandments the way they did when the Bible plainly stated that they were actually given by God Himself and written down with God's own finger? No one had the right to modify what God had declared.

Not only did Jack feel deeply hurt and betrayed—he was angry. As soon as possible he went to the Catholic chaplain and said, "I don't understand about this change."

The chaplain sighed. "Jack, don't you understand about the church's authority on earth?" The priest then did his best to explain how the Roman Catholic Church felt God had ordained it to modify understanding of Scripture to meet new conditions. Jack didn't accept his explanation.

"How can mere human beings have *any* right to change what God has written on stone with His own finger?"

The pain of confronting the priest with his questions was unnerving and nearly shattered Jack's religious fervor. He had been brought up Catholic—baptized, confirmed, served as an altar boy, and, although he had forsaken his church for a period, he now considered himself a good Catholic. His spiritual foundations seemed to be crumbling beneath him as he listened to the priest. Until then it had never occurred to him how much he depended on the church for salvation.

"Well, what God says is more important than what any church says, and that's that!" Jack concluded as he left the chaplain's office.

Returning to his barrack, he searched for more about the Sabbath in his *Bible Readings for the Home Circle*. In it he discovered that the Sabbath is a sign between God and His people indicating that they belong to Him (Eze. 20:12). That made sense. Jack wanted everyone to know that he belonged to God, so he made up his mind that he would keep the Sabbath, even if he were the only one to do so. He set about to observe God's Sabbath the best way he could, regardless of the consequences.

Since Carl had a different work schedule and they had little or no regular contact with each other, Jack knew that whatever happened about Sabbaths, he would have to make his own arrangements independent of what Carl did or did not do. After praying about it, Jack went to his officer to request Sabbaths off.

To say the experience was not easy is a profound understatement. The officer in charge was a militant Christian and minister of music at a large church on the base. "The Air Force recognizes Sunday as the Lord's day, not Saturday," was his uncompromising, matter-of-fact response to Jack's request.

"So who is the Air Force to recognize Sunday as the Lord's day when the Bible plainly states that Saturday is the Sabbath?" Jack asked incredulously. "The entire Armed Forces can't change what God says, no matter how hard they try!"

"You can't take everything you read in the Bible so literally, Private. You'll drive yourself crazy. I can probably get you Sundays off if you're that obsessed with it."

"I don't need Sundays off."

"Private, do you drink?"

"No, not anymore, I don't."

"What would you do if you were in the middle of the desert, and there was nothing to drink but beer?"

"I don't know the answer to your question, sir. All I know is that no one can change God's commandments, which He wrote with His own finger—not the Catholic Church, who claims to have changed it; not the Protestant church, who follows their lead; and certainly not the Air Force, who doesn't even recognize a plain statement from Scripture that says the Sabbath is the Lord's holy day!"

"We're not getting anywhere," the officer finally snarled angrily after a lengthy period of bantering. "You'll have to see the commanding officer."

"Fine. Do you set that up, or do I?"

The commanding officer turned out to be a very pleasant fellow, easy to talk to and open to views differing from his own. After Jack explained his convictions, the commander turned to the previous officer and said, "If this man wants his Sabbath off, let him have it. He must make his own arrangements in switching shifts with others, but as long as he does that, then he can go to church if he wants to."

Convinced of the necessity to obey God's command, Jack had been ready to face court-martial if necessary. However, he didn't realize how difficult switching shifts would be. Every time he found himself scheduled to work either Friday night or Saturday (which was almost every week), he had to find someone willing to trade shifts with him. Often it was late Friday afternoon before he located someone to work that night or the next day in exchange for his taking a Sunday shift. The next year and a half tested his faith and his commitment to the Sabbath, but the Lord always worked things out.

After talking with the priest, Jack thought that he probably was no longer a good Catholic, but he didn't really know what to believe, so he sent away for a book called *A Faith for You,* which supposedly described all Christian groups. He read it, searching for a church that truly followed the Bible. Scores of churches had their basic beliefs listed in the book, but the more he read, the more confused he became. There were so many similarities, yet so many differences. He didn't know what to do.

Ultimately, he decided to simply follow the Lord and keep His commandments, even if he were the only one in the world doing it. That much he knew was right. Hadn't he just read that God required nothing but "to do justly, and to love mercy, and to walk humbly with God" (Micah 6:8)? He didn't know much theologically, but he knew God well enough to realize that if he loved Him with all his heart and did his best to keep His commandments, God would guide him.

The migraine headaches had greatly subsided with Jack's improved health habits, but he still had occasional bouts with them even though he carefully avoided every food or drink he connected with their occurrence. However, the headaches remained a mystery to the doctors, who had now decided to send Jack back to the States for more extensive medical treatment.

Then one night in a dream Jack saw some texts. Of course, he was still reading in the Old Testament, not having gotten beyond the minor prophets, but the references he saw so vividly were Matthew 7:7, 8 and Matthew 8:7. Numerous times they flashed before him in his dream. When he awoke the next morning, the dream was still fresh in his mind, so he immediately looked them up since he had no idea what the verses said.

The first passage, Matthew 7:7 and 8, said, "Ask, and it shall be given you; seek, and ye shall find; knock, and it shall be opened unto you: for every one that asketh receiveth; and he that seeketh findeth; and to him that knocketh it shall be opened."

"Well," he mused, "this is obviously talking about prayer. But what does it have to do with me?"

So he turned to the next text, Matthew 8:7: "And Jesus saith unto him, I will come and heal him."

Is God trying to tell me something? Could it be that He will heal me if I ask Him? Immediately, Jack began praying to be healed of his headaches. Miraculously, he never had another migraine headache the remainder of his time in Guam. Later, he reflected that God could just as well have allowed him to return to the States for healing. But then he would have missed the experience of solitude, time to study, and the mission emphasis he gained on Guam that helped set a pattern for the rest of his life.

Carl had finished his Bible correspondence lessons and was regularly attending the Seventh-day Adventist church on Guam. Ray Turner, a former member of the Voice of Prophecy's King's Heralds quartet, was the mission evangelist. Since Carl was seriously considering baptism, he invited Jack to church with him at Dededo and introduced him to Pastor Ray. Pastor Ray always invited Carl and Jack to his home and to potlucks, socials, and other occasions. Jack felt comfortable with the friendly, accepting group. Often he would be with the church members all evening, then return to the base just in time to work the night shift. He enjoyed the warm Christian fellowship. Once he discovered that he was not the only one observing the Sabbath, that thousands of others everywhere around the globe did also, he said to himself, *Why not belong to a church in which we can all encourage each other?*

The Korean War soon escalated to the point where everyone on Guam was put on alert. Jack had never prayed so hard for anything in his life as that he would not have to go to Korea. He had only about six months left to his assignment in Guam, and he strongly felt he had seen enough war at close range in his brief life. "Lord, please don't let them pick me," he pleaded. Through some military quirk, Carl went, but Jack did not. Because they had become such close friends, even that was hard to take.

Carl decided to be baptized before leaving Guam, and he invited Jack to join him in taking that step. When Pastor Turner questioned Jack, he found that the Holy Spirit had already led him into believing everything that Seventh-day Adventists taught as far as lifestyle was involved: he was already paying tithe, believed in Ellen White's inspiration, and had been observing the Sabbath. The only thing he needed instruction on was the sanctuary doctrine, which he happily studied from the Bible and fully believed. Since there was nothing to hold him back, Jack decided to go ahead and be baptized with Carl. He wrote a hurried letter home, telling his mother of the wonderful changes in his life, about how God had marvelously answered his prayer about not having to go to Korea, and about his upcoming baptism later that week.

The Sabbath afternoon scene at Suicide Cliff (where so many Japanese had died for their country by jumping off it rather than surrender) was a fitting symbol of the young airmen's commitment to their Lord. In a quiet lagoon of the blue Pacific with believers singing about the love of Jesus from the shore, Carl and Jack were baptized.

Chapter Fourteen

Not Ashamed

After Carl shipped out for Korea, Jack felt extremely lonely. Who knew when or if they would ever see each other again? He had had so few really good friends with whom he had anything in common that Carl's departure left Jack feeling depressed. More and more he turned to his Bible.

Then calamity struck. He had been waiting impatiently for a letter from his mother in response to his about the wonderful things God had been doing in his life. When the anticipated letter at last arrived, Jack joyfully hurried to his bunk to read it. He knew that his mother would be pleased that he had found God again at last! She would rejoice that God had turned his life around and now he desired only to do God's will. Jack could hardly wait to actually read her delighted response. But the very first line was a surprising and stinging rebuke.

> Dear Jack,
>
> I cannot believe that you are even considering being baptized into a Protestant church. If you do go through with this wild notion, please don't ever plan to come to our home again. You will not be welcome at our house and should never expect to eat at our table . . .
>
> Can you not understand what a terrible disgrace this brings to our family? What will your aunts and

> uncles think? You know that joining a Protestant church is strictly forbidden. It is a dreadful curse on the entire family, worse than an infectious disease. I will be blamed for all you have done, for not instructing and raising you in the way of the church. Your grandparents will be shocked and angry.
>
> Everyone has done so much for you, and now, by becoming a Protestant, you are turning against the whole family, as well as God. It simply cannot be. I will not have it, at least not in my home! Think through very carefully what you are doing.

The letter ended abruptly. Jack was stunned and confused. He couldn't believe his own mother would turn against him. Would his family reject him because he loved and obeyed God? His mother had not even mentioned her gratitude to God for keeping him from going to Korea. Jack was so thankful for that blessing that he praised God every day. He had expected his mother to at least mention it.

Lying on his bunk, he thought things over, remembering how his grandparents had felt about Protestants. Grandfather had always shown respect for them, tipping his hat when he passed their church or cemetery, but that was about it. For a Catholic to become a Protestant was in his relatives' eyes like being a traitor to one's country.

Does my family really expect me to deny my newfound faith? Jack wondered. A text came forcefully to his mind: "No man, having put his hand to the plough, and looking back, is fit for the kingdom of God" (Luke 9:62). The passage was especially meaningful, since he had spent many years plowing. Grandfather had taught him to hold on to the plow firmly, put his weight against it, and keep his eyes focused on a marker ahead. There simply was no way to plow a straight furrow if one kept glancing back. His decision was made. Jack could not, would not, look back.

The next day Jack wrote to his mother, telling her that he had already been baptized. He poured out his love for her, his appreciation for her guidance and prayers, his vow that he would always love her, no matter what, even if she never wanted to see him again. Then, after mailing the letter, he decided to write her every single day. Surely, his mother's obvious strong love for him would win out over her prejudice.

But Jack did not realize how staunchly loyal his mother was to her church and how faithful she was to what she had been taught. He did not know the pressure she faced from family and friends, not to mention the priest. No letter came back in reply. Weeks went by. Then months. Jack continued to write her daily.

He kept busy at the Adventist mission whenever he had time off. With so much free time on his hands, he read all the Ellen White books the little church had and soaked up the Adventist lifestyle. The time spent with church employees and believers on the tiny island of Guam was an education in itself, and his avid reading stood him in good stead when he was later able to go to college and prepare for the ministry. It would help him maintain a balanced view on numerous theological problems that later arose in the ministry and the Adventist educational system.

Throwing himself into Pathfinder activities, Jack became a Master Guide. He accompanied the young people on their singing bands and helped maintain the church buildings, painting and doing other maintenance jobs. In fact, he became so involved in church activities that he appealed to the commander of the base to allow him to stay in Guam until his enlistment was up. Jack wanted to be discharged right there, then stay and work for the mission. Was this the same person who when he first arrived couldn't wait to get off the island? However, the base commander refused his request. He must go back to the States and be discharged there.

After almost six months of writing to his mother about his daily activities, his disappointments, his hopes, his dreams, and his strong faith in God, Jack finally received a letter back from her. It was brief but not so hostile.

"Jack," she wrote, "when you get your leave, it would be good to see you, but I'm sure you understand that you cannot actually stay at our house."

Well, at least that was something. Perhaps she would soften more. He would keep praying and writing.

As time for Jack's departure from Guam drew nearer, he thought about how he could prepare the way for his mother to receive the Advent message that he was sure, if she only studied, she would embrace. He never thought about how she would work out a Sabbath-free schedule in the restaurant business. In fact, Jack was so absorbed with Christ that he thought little about any problems involved in observing the Sabbath. To him it was a simple matter. If you loved God, you obeyed Him. God would take care of the rest.

Then an idea struck him. *I'll find the address of a Chicago church and ask if the pastor will visit Mother and invite her to church.*

The answer to his letter told him that a Bible instructor would be happy to visit Katie Blanco. Jack prayed that his mother would be led to accept an invitation to worship with the Adventist believers in Chicago.

Some time later he received a letter from the Bible instructor. "Your mother was very gracious and polite, but she seemed totally disinterested in any religion other than her own. When I prepared to leave, she surprised me by handing me some money for visiting and praying with her. Of course, I declined, but she was so insistent that I finally took it and told her I would see that it went to a good cause." Jack could almost visualize the scene, knowing that giving money was a custom Catholics followed when the priest visited and prayed for them. The letter went on, "I'm sorry I was unable to begin giving her Bible studies. It would really have been lovely if your mother had been interested enough to study and be ready for baptism when you return, as you suggested. But perhaps the Holy Spirit has a different timetable."

Terribly disappointed, Jack in his naiveté had assumed that his mother would be as eager to follow Jesus as he had been, eager to learn more about His will for her life. It was hard for him to comprehend the impact of so many years of being steeped in the catechism, Mass, confession, and other activities of the church.

Then he had another idea. *No one knows Mother like I do. Perhaps the Bible instructor did not approach her right. I'll take up the challenge when I get home.*

Jack tossed the letter from the Bible instructor into the trash behind the barracks. On second thought, he decided maybe he should save the address in case he needed it later, so he retrieved the envelope, tore off the return address, and stuffed it into his wallet.

Jack talked to the Adventist missionaries about his situation. "If Mother won't listen to me," he said, "then I'll go from door-to-door, from town-to-town, and tell everybody the good news I have found. I can't believe that anyone would not want to know how much God loves them!" But the church leaders advised him that a better course would be to go to college and prepare for the ministry.

Letters from Mother came more frequently now, and she seemed at last to have had a slight change of heart. Now it appeared that she was looking forward to Jack's return home and planned for him to stay with them at their house as long as he was on furlough. He took that as a sign that the Holy Spirit was already working in her life.

When at last the time of his furlough and reassignment came, he boarded a ship for San Francisco. Approaching the Golden Gate Bridge was almost as thrilling as seeing the Statue of Liberty some years before. As soon as the ship docked in the harbor and he got located on the Air Force base, Jack headed for the bus station and bought a ticket to Chicago. He had to see his mother as soon as possible and start telling her in person about his joy in Christ and the wonderful changes it had brought to his life.

Mother was genuinely happy to see him, and she expressed delight that he had given up drinking and smoking. Eagerly Jack tried to tell his mother everything about his new life. She was gracious and polite, though she obviously wondered if her son had taken leave of his senses. She said the vegetarian part was a little bizarre.

"It was bad enough to change your day of worship," she said, "when you know good and well that, as mother of all churches, the Catholic Church could not possibly be wrong. But to quit eating meat—why, that's ridiculous!"

Jack tried to explain that it was a health principle. "Mother, you know yourself that the Catholic Church forbids eating meat on Friday, which is really dumb because there's no reason for it, other than it's a church edict." All during his leave he refused to eat meat of any kind, much to his mother's inevitable disgust.

When other relatives came to celebrate his homecoming, Jack, thinking he was witnessing to them, passed up all the dishes that his aunts and cousins had prepared especially for him. Later, he realized that he had hurt everyone's feelings, and he sincerely wished he had not made such an issue of it. Maybe they would have listened to some other things he had to tell them if they had not considered him such a fanatic on that score.

"Mother," Jack asked on Friday, "do you know where there is a Seventh-day Adventist church?"

Obviously confused, she asked, "What's *that?*" Apparently, the fact that Jack had become a Protestant overshadowed the identification of exactly what specific denomination he had embraced.

"That's the church I attend now," Jack answered.

"You know, Jack, there was a nice young woman who came and wanted to study the Bible with me. She was from that church—very pleasant." His mother paused, then teased,

"You ought to get better acquainted with her—she might be a good match for you."

His mouth dropped open. Certainly not interested in marriage, he planned to live a celibate life, as Jesus had. It surprised him that his mother knew that the Bible instructor was an Adventist. If she really opposed Adventists so much, why would she suggest that he get interested in an Adventist girl?

"Well," Jack grinned, "she must have really been something to impress you that much."

Normally, he would have looked in the phone book and chosen a church from the many listed. But since he still had the Bible instructor's name and address in his wallet, he called her to get the location of her church. Actually, Jack had been spoiled at the mission because someone had always been willing and eager to transport the Adventist military men back and forth to church activities. However, instead of offering to pick him up, the Bible instructor gave him directions, told him which streetcar to catch, and what time services started.

Jack pulled his Air Force hat as close to his ears as possible against the winter's sting and caught the streetcar to church. Because he was early and in uniform, the Bible instructor spotted him sitting in the pew as soon as she came in. The attractive, petite young woman approached and introduced herself. "You must be Jack," she smiled. "I'm Marion Blasius, the Bible instructor who visited your mother." She was friendly, but most professional in her demeanor.

Mother had a point! Jack mused to himself. But he immediately asked Marion about her visit with his mother.

"Your mother was most cordial," the young woman answered, "but she showed no interest at all in studying even the Catholic Bible. We mostly talked about you. After we had prayer and I was ready to leave, she insisted I take some money for my church. That was the only visit I had with her because she so obviously was not ready to listen to a Protestant talk about the Bible."

Even though Marion had written all this earlier in a letter, it was still disappointing to hear it again firsthand. "Well, I really do appreciate your trying," Jack said. "Thanks a lot."

Marion introduced him to the pastor and then excused herself to go to take up her responsibilities of greeting others at the door. After church Jack spotted her and asked, "What are you doing this afternoon?"

"I'm giving a Bible study."

"Would you mind if I came along? I'd like to learn more about giving Bible studies."

"OK," she replied. "Oh, Mother," she turned to a gracious older woman, "this is Jack Blanco, who is a new Adventist home on leave from Guam." Marion's mother took pity on the Adventist serviceman and invited him to their home for Sabbath dinner.

The Pathfinders were to participate in a conference-wide event the following day, but had not mastered how to pivot. The leader asked them to remain after church for a brief practice in marching. Spotting Jack's uniform, the leader asked if he would mind staying a few minutes to help teach them.

Mrs. Blasius drove home to prepare dinner, and following the Pathfinder practice, Jack and Marion took a streetcar to their apartment. The afternoon flew by quickly, and being January in Chicago, it was soon sundown. It had been one of the best days of Jack's life. Then, to cap it all off, Mrs. Blasius invited Jack to go with them to a program out at the nearby academy. Life was indeed good.

CHAPTER FIFTEEN

Courting

Since Jack had almost a month of furlough to spend in Chicago and he was eager to get to work for the Lord, he volunteered his services to the church. He particularly wanted to share his faith by giving Bible studies, beginning with his own mother and stepfather.

Marion located a film projector for him and showed him how to use the Bible study filmstrips. In his enthusiasm he felt that two studies at a time would be far more effective than the single one that Marion recommended. Besides, he was eager to complete them all before he had to leave for his final military assignment. Strangely enough, after the first session, everyone began to have "other appointments" or "headaches" or offered some other excuse to not be present. Jack sadly realized they were politely saying, "No thanks."

Intense and undaunted in his "witnessing," he went to the health food store and bought some vegetarian hot dogs. When his parents tasted them, they looked at each other rather strangely, swallowed with some difficulty, and remarked, "These are, uh, 'different'!" The strange expression on their faces made him decide to eat them himself and not press his luck. After all, they were trying to be courteous.

As he realized later, he was entirely too zealous in wanting his mother to know and understand everything as he did. He continued to force-feed religion to her until she had an unbearable case of spiritual indigestion. She soon became literally nauseous at the mention of certain subjects.

One afternoon he overheard her talking to a neighbor. "I don't know what in the world to do about Jack and his crazy new religion!"

"Well, Katie, I suspect that after all he's been through, both in Germany and then in the Air Force," the woman suggested, "he's probably suffering from something like shell shock. I'll bet in time he'll recover and go back to his old religion. Don't worry so about it. Those things have a way of working out."

The next Sabbath when Jack came home after church all was quiet, since everyone was at work. He was able to get out his Bible and read as much as he wanted for a while. Later in the afternoon his stepfather came in to rest a bit and switched on the TV before collapsing on the couch. Television was still new, and Jack had never had to cope with it before. The noise and confusion made it so difficult to concentrate on his Sabbath reading that he decided to go out for a walk.

As he walked, it dawned on him that no one in his family was the least bit interested in what he felt was the most important issue in life. Never had he suffered any pain as intense as that of seeing those he loved most seemingly rejecting the grace of his loving Father. If there was something he was doing wrong in trying to convey God's love, he sincerely wanted to correct it. He decided to ask an expert. Soon he was on the phone with Marion, the Bible instructor.

"Would you mind if I went with you when you give your next Bible study? I must be doing something wrong, because no one wants to listen to me."

Marion agreed for Jack to accompany her to her next study, but she would be leaving right away. "Can you be ready when I get there?"

Before long, she arrived in her new 1950 Plymouth. It was late January and the snow was deep and the roads icy. It was also bitter cold as Jack ran from his front door and jumped into the front seat beside her. As Marion drove away from Jack's house and rounded the first corner, the car slid helplessly into the curb.

"Oh, no!" Marion exclaimed, embarrassed beyond words.

But Jack was jubilant at his chance to play hero. He managed to push the car while Marion steered it back onto the street. They even got to the study on time. The young woman was so appreciative of his help that it almost made him feel guilty.

As far as Jack was concerned, the Bible study was a huge success. Watching Marion in action as she carefully and considerately explained various Bible texts to the interested people gave Jack a special thrill. Truly she was as dedicated to the Lord as he was. Going to Bible studies together became a daily occurrence. Because of the winter weather, Marion deferred to Jack as the chauffeur. He hardly dared to encourage the thought that was taking root in his mind.

That Saturday night the church had a social, and Jack managed to spend at least part of the evening with Marion. She was reserved, not wishing to set tongues wagging nor to neglect anyone with whom she was studying.

Talking with Marion from time to time over the next several days, he often referred to some treasured quotation from the writings of Ellen White. "Where did you read that?" she would question.

"Give me [whatever book it was], and I'll show you." Then he would quickly leaf through the pages and locate it.

Marion had worked as a reader for the chairman of the Religion Department in college, but Jack seemed to have a better grasp of theology and religious principles than most religion majors. "How do you remember where you've read all those things?" she asked incredulously.

"Well, I read them so recently," he dismissed her wonder at his keen memory. "After reading the Bible through for the Master Guide requirement, I just bought one book at a time until I had finished all the major ones."

"All in one year? You should be a preacher!"

Jack grinned. "That's what people tell me. I'd really like to get a job where there are no Adventists and raise up a church. Then move to another place, get another job, and establish another church. Wouldn't that be rewarding!"

"And what would happen to the people you left behind?" she asked. "Jack, you really ought to think about working for the church full-time. You know, you would be paid to win and nurture souls."

She left the thought to take root. Jack's leave was almost over, and it was about time to head to McCord Air Force Base in Tacoma, Washington, his new post. Marion told him that her former pastor from the Chicago church, DeWitt Osgood, had recently moved to Tacoma. She asked Jack to convey special greetings to him, which he promised to do. Elder Osgood had been like a father to her during his ministry in Chicago after her own father had left the family.

The morning of his departure Jack finished packing his things and was about to phone his mother at work for a last goodbye when he felt a strong conviction to telephone Marion also. First he rejected the thought because he really had already told her goodbye. As he continued packing, the conviction came again. Then a third time. It almost seemed that a voice urged, "Call her. You need to say goodbye again."

Marion had been delayed that morning as she planned her visitation schedule for the day. She was just heading out when the phone rang. "I thought you had already left," she laughed when Jack said hello. "I was just heading out to make some calls on evangelistic interests. Did you need something?"

He admitted he didn't know why he had called. "Just thought I'd like to talk to you again before leaving."

She promised to swing by his house. Hurriedly finishing packing, Jack called his mother for a last goodbye, then went down to meet Marion. They drove to the University of Chicago and parked on the boulevard. Turning, she asked, "Now what did you want to see me about? Your mother, perhaps?"

"Marion, I really appreciate what you and your mother have done for me since I've been home—taking in a total stranger like you have. You've given me valuable lessons in how to share my faith and be gracious and kind and not so overzealous." Then, before Jack knew it, he stammered, "I've really grown to admire you, Marion, and your relationship with God. I think He might have brought us together for a reason. I'd really like for us to keep up our friendship. Would you be willing to stay in contact by mail?"

Marion was speechless. He was asking her to continue their friendship—a courtship?—by mail. After an embarrassing silence, she answered, "Frankly, Jack, I really don't think this will work."

"What do you mean? Is there some reason?" Jack reached for her hand. "I really do think a lot of you already, Marion."

"Well, for one thing, I've already finished college, and you've hardly begun. We're at different points in our lives. Besides, I'm just not ready for a serious relationship." She gently pulled her hand away and told him again that she simply did not think it would work. Finally, though, she agreed to write. And yes, she certainly would pray about the matter. She suggested again that he talk to Elder Osgood in Tacoma and seek his advice. Then they prayed together, and Marion drove Jack back to his apartment.

In one way, Jack felt a bit deflated at her obvious lack of interest, yet in another way, he was walking on air. At least, she hadn't totally turned down his request that they write. It was a start.

CHAPTER SIXTEEN

Testing Time

When Jack arrived at the base in Tacoma, he immediately began having trouble getting Sabbaths free. His new sergeant gave him a hard time from the start, cursing with every breath. "You're nothing but a religious fanatic! You don't join the Air Force and then tell them when you'll work and when you won't. You could be court-martialed. We can't possibly give everyone Saturdays off. Don't be such an idiot!" Expletives peppered each derogatory sentence, and, try as he would, Jack could get nowhere.

Finally, insisting on an appeal to the base commander, Jack received permission, and went to see the top man accompanied by his belligerent sergeant. After another long tirade about Jack being a troublesome fanatic trying to use the Bible to get his own way to meet his own ends, the sergeant ran out of steam.

"OK, Private, what's your story?" The commander turned his chair and focused full attention on Jack.

"Sir, I'm requesting Saturdays off because the Bible says the seventh day is the day that God pronounced holy. He said we're not supposed to work on that day. Sir, I have finally come to understand the importance of obeying God, and I'm requesting permission from the Air Force to obey God's command to rest on the Sabbath and keep His day holy." Fear seemed to have vanished, and Jack's words spilled out without conscious effort.

The commander tapped his pencil eraser on his desk as Jack talked. "And you think that day is Saturday," he said without emotion.

"Yes, sir. From Creation it was kept, down through Moses' time when God gave the Ten Commandments. Jesus observed it and the disciples, and Isaiah even says it will be the day of worship in heaven."

"You realize, of course, what kind of problem a request like yours causes in the military?" The officer carefully avoided being drawn into any religious debate on biblical interpretation.

"Yes, sir. But I would be willing to work on Saturday if there was a genuine emergency. For instance, if there were only two communication operators available, and the other man got sick. But surely there are lots of guys who would be happy to have me work for them on Sundays."

The commander listened patiently to everything Jack had to say. Then he turned to the sergeant. "This man is not a fanatic. In fact, he appears to be quite reasonable. I want you to see that he gets every Saturday off, and put it on the schedule. Is that clear?"

Although overjoyed, Jack did not dare risk a glance at the sergeant, and he tried not to smile too broadly as he gratefully thanked the commander. Again he had fully expected to be court-martialed, but the Holy Spirit had worked on the commander's heart in his behalf. The sergeant, though, managed to get his revenge. Even though Jack had more seniority than others in his unit and a perfect record, he was completely passed over for promotion at least twice. That intentional slight hurt, but Jack reasoned that it was a small price to pay for the freedom to follow what the Scriptures indicated.

It was hard to leave base without a car, but he did call Pastor Osgood, as Marion had suggested, and asked how to get to the Tacoma church. The minister invited the young airman to his home, welcoming him as his own son when he arrived, but Jack did not mention Marion. After a brief and friendly chat,

Osgood gave him directions to the church and a schedule of the various meetings and activities, along with an enthusiastic invitation and welcome.

Daily Jack wrote to Marion, and it was always a special highlight when mail arrived from her. Though her letters were not as frequent, their friendship deepened as they expressed to each other their love for Jesus and shared more of their personal lives. Then Marion wrote that she felt that their relationship might be getting too serious.

"Jack," her letter said, "why don't you talk to Elder Osgood and find out if he would advise us to continue corresponding." Because Jack was such a recent convert, she no doubt wondered if he might drift out of the church, since he had no family to encourage him. Unknown to Jack, at one time Pastor Osgood had told her, "I'll be interested in meeting the man you decide to marry." She had full confidence in the pastor's commitment to God, his judgment, and his tactful diplomacy in spiritually nurturing his members. But still Jack delayed in mentioning her when he talked with the pastor.

One day Pastor Osgood called him. "Say, Jack, I was wondering if you would be willing to share your conversion story at the Sabbath afternoon young people's meeting next week?"

It was the first time anyone had ever asked Jack to speak in public, yet somehow he was not nervous. After all, he would simply be talking about his friend Jesus. He really wanted others to love Him, too. And he determined that after the meeting, he would speak to Pastor Osgood about Marion and their growing friendship and ask his advice, as she had suggested. Since the minister would pick him up and return him to the base, surely he would have a chance during the ride back to mention what was on his heart.

After the young people's meeting, Elder Osgood put his arm around Jack's shoulder and said warmly, "I really appreciate you sharing your experience. Your love and commitment to Jesus is obviously earnest and sincere. You were a real blessing and encouragement to our young people."

Jack wanted to tell him about Marion right then, but somehow it didn't seem appropriate. He wondered if the pastor might advise that a brash new Christian with such a cloudy past should forget courting such a dedicated young woman as Marion. As Jack got into the pastor's car, he said, "I really would like to talk to you. Do you have a little extra time today?"

"Certainly," the pastor answered. "Let's stop at my house so we can discuss things in a quiet place."

It wasn't long until they were seated in the pastor's study, and Elder Osgood opened the conversation. "Jack, what do you plan to do with your life when you leave the military?"

"Well, Pastor, I hope you don't think I'm being presumptuous, but I really feel that God might be calling me to the ministry."

"Why, Jack, I'm very glad to hear that!" He gave an approving nod. Then he added, "You know, there's a fine young lady back in Chicago I really wish you could meet. Her name is Marion Blasius. She's a Bible instructor, and a very dedicated one, I might add." Then he began apologizing, "Forgive me if I come across as a matchmaker. It's definitely not my practice to do that. But if the Lord should lead you in the direction of marriage . . ." He didn't finish the sentence before asking, "Have you ever met Marion?"

Jack's mouth had dropped open. Then a smile spread from ear to ear. When he found his voice, he said, "That's exactly what I came to see you about, Pastor."

He then told Elder Osgood, "Not only do I know who Marion is, but I have gone with her on numerous occasions to give Bible studies, and I'm currently corresponding with her."

Now it was the pastor's turn to be surprised. "I didn't know that you were even acquainted with Marion. You could easily have slipped in and out of a Chicago church without ever meeting her. And you've never mentioned her, not even in your story at the young people's meeting!"

"Now I've not actually proposed to her," Jack explained, "but there's beginning to be sort of an understanding."

"Well, let's not consider our conversation to necessarily be a sign of the Lord's leading," Elder Osgood smiled. He then advised, "Jack, you need to pray twice as much as before that the Lord will lead, and if it's His will for you two to become more serious, to make it evident, and if not, to make that evident as well."

To Jack the entire conversation seemed providential, but he knew that one could, as Pastor Osgood had suggested, also misinterpret such incidents. But he could hardly wait to telephone Marion. After relaying the conversation he had had with the pastor, he suggested, "If it's OK with you, I'd like to come to Chicago to see you soon. Hopefully we can then decide one way or another about our relationship."

Marion agreed, and Jack hastily made plans to take 10 days of accumulated leave in April. Then he phoned his mother and told her what he planned to do. She was extremely distressed.

"Jack, when I suggested that Marion was a fine girl and you ought to get better acquainted with her, I was really only kidding. I never dreamed it would turn out like this! Not that I have anything against Marion personally, you understand, but I had hoped all along that you would return to your senses and become a faithful Catholic again. If you marry a Seventh-day Adventist girl, it will probably mean that you will stay with that crazy religion. I hate to think what that will mean for you ultimately."

"Mother," Jack continued when she finally paused, "I plan to go to college . . ."

"That's good. I'm glad to hear that!"

" . . . and study to be a minister."

"What? Jack, this is *too* much!" She put her husband on the phone after a muffled discussion with him.

Concern filled his stepfather's voice. "Jack, if you really want to go to college, we'll be glad to send you wherever you choose to go—Yale, Harvard, Princeton—anywhere. You can take law, medicine, business, whatever you wish. We'll pay your full tuition. But you will have to give up this foolish notion of going into the ministry of a Protestant church. I'm afraid that would be the death of your mother."

But Jack had heard the call of God, and their offer, though appreciated, held no interest for him. Also, his plans definitely included Marion, if she would have him.

This time he took the train home instead of the bus because he was eager to be with her as much as possible. When it finally pulled into the Chicago station, the most beautiful girl he had ever seen was happily waving to him. From her warm welcome he sensed that she, too, was glad to be continuing their courtship in person for the brief time they had.

Marion had arranged to have vacation time off while Jack was home, and the two young people spent as much time together as possible. "How would you like to drive to Michigan to visit Wilma, my former college roommate?" she asked. "She's married to a pastor. I'd like to get more counsel on our future plans from someone not so involved."

Jack agreed, and decided to check out Emmanuel Missionary College. He would soon have to make a decision where he would continue schooling after his discharge. Before the end of their brief stay, Marion received her friend's enthusiastic blessing on the relationship.

On the way back to Chicago, Jack said, "You know, Marion, from every evidence, I believe God appears to be leading us in the direction of marriage."

But Marion still hesitated. In spite of approval from her former pastor and close friends, the decision to marry was difficult. Her own parents had gone through a painful divorce, and she would rather never marry than to endure such pain again. Since she wanted to make sure that the Lord Himself was leading, they decided to continue to correspond and pray for wisdom to discern God's will.

When the furlough ended, Marion took Jack to the train station for a tearful goodbye. They had truly grown to love each other. As the train lurched noisily away, Jack clung to the railing outside the train car, watching her petite figure grow smaller and smaller in the distance. Suddenly he felt exactly as he had so many years ago in Germany when his mother had left to go to the States without him. A dark cloud of doubt and foreboding settled over him. It was, he felt, the beginning of a long and painful separation and perhaps the end of their friendship.

But love for his heavenly Father was even stronger than human relationships, and whatever was *His* will was the only important consideration. Jack tried to hold back the tears, but it was impossible. He found a seat to himself, turned toward the window, and wept inconsolably until finally no more tears came.

Almost immediately upon his return to Washington, he received a letter from Marion. "When your train pulled away," she wrote, "I felt as if my heart were being physically torn out. I'll have to admit to crying for a very long time."

That letter restored his hope for their future together. But he said nothing to Elder Osgood about his leave or how their courtship had progressed, and the pastor didn't ask.

For weeks the couple continued corresponding and praying about their relationship until they felt the time had come to seek more advice from their pastor friend. "Jack, why don't you find out—if we *should* decide to marry—would Elder Osgood be willing to perform the wedding?" Marion suggested. What she really wanted was advice from a godly man who knew both of them. They agreed that the pastor's approval of their union would be the sign from the Lord for which they had been praying.

Jack made an appointment to talk to Elder Osgood. Walking up the hill to the familiar home, he sensed an overwhelming conviction that the response would be negative. That's the way most things seemed to go in his life, so he braced for it. And how could they expect a minister in Washington State to travel all the way to Chicago for a wedding? They could not even offer to pay his travel expenses. It *was* pretty presumptuous, he decided. When Jack reached the door, Elder Osgood welcomed him warmly and invited him into his study.

"Well, how did your trip to Chicago go? I've not known whether I should ask!" the pastor began jovially.

Jack eagerly told about his visit, and then with a prayer in his heart that somehow it would be the Lord's will, he stammered, "Elder Osgood, is there any chance that you would be able to come to Chicago and marry us? I—I mean, do you think we are suited for each other?"

"Why, Jack," the older man smiled, "it just happens that I'll be going through Chicago the latter part of September on my way to Fall Council. If that timing works, I'd be honored to perform a wedding ceremony for you two."

Jack's face lit up. "Really?"

Now all he had to do was to get Marion to agree to marry him in September. As soon as he could get to a telephone, he called her. She was pleased at Elder Osgood's endorsement of the idea. Her answer to Jack's "official" proposal was a delighted but subdued, "Yes, Jack." After a lengthy conversation about arrangements, he offered a prayer of thanksgiving over the phone, committing their lives to God's service.

As soon as he was off the phone, he shouted for joy. They had set the date for September 28. Immediately he went to put in a request for his remaining two weeks of furlough. Marion turned in her resignation to the Illinois Conference so they would have plenty of time to find her replacement.

In spite of all they had to do, it seemed that summer would never end. Finally, in late September Jack flew back to Chicago. Marion met him at the airport. They enjoyed a lingering embrace and kissed each other on the cheeks—since Jack didn't think kissing on the lips proper until *after* the ceremony. Well, that was now less than a week away.

CHAPTER SEVENTEEN

Man and Wife

The wedding day dawned sunny and beautiful. Because the Adventists were temporarily using a Congregational church, the wedding could not begin until after the Sunday morning services ended. Mrs. Blasius insisted that the scores of out-of-town guests must be served dinner in the fellowship hall at 5:00 p.m., regardless of the 7:00 p.m. wedding.

Jack greeted dozens of people he did not know. Marion felt equally overwhelmed. Neither had time or opportunity to be hungry. The four bridesmaids were busy helping everywhere. Everyone had so much to do and so little time. Wilma, the maid of honor, reminded Marion it was time to hurry to her mother's apartment to change into their wedding clothes.

Exhausted, but exuberant, Jack was finally able to pull away to change into his tuxedo. "Six forty-five," his best man said with a glance at his watch. "They'll be getting back here soon—and we'd better be ready, if I know anything about brides."

The other groomsmen laughed, totally unaware of what had been happening across town at the bride's house.

"Oh, *no!*" Marion had wailed as the car stopped at her apartment. "Wilma, I don't have the house key with me. We can't even get in to change!" The church was several miles away, and many frantic minutes passed before they returned with her mother's key. "How could I have been so careless?" she fretted.

"Everything's OK, Marion," Wilma soothed. *"All* weddings

start late. This will just give you something special to remember about this day. Don't worry so—this will just prove you're fashionable!"

Meanwhile, back at the church, 10-year-old Marie asked, "Do I look all right, Mama," as she swung around for at least the tenth time in her lavender junior bridesmaid dress. Wondrously, because of Marion's warm and loving ways of including her, even Katie approved of the marriage. Elder Osgood was there to officiate, accompanied by Wayne White, the current Chicago pastor. Brad Braley was prepared to begin playing the organ as soon as the bride arrived. But she didn't.

Soon all the seats filled and more people filtered in to stand at the back of the sanctuary. Guests would never know that Jack and Dad Blasius had spent the previous evening building steps up to the rostrum. Or that Marion's uncle Lawrence had provided the white aisle cloth (since he was in the awning business). Or that Uncle Jack was supplying the bountiful wedding cake for the reception. Or even that Marion's bridal gown had been borrowed from a cousin. However, they all *did* know that the wedding was a bit late getting started.

Finally, the music began, a relieved Jack entered from a side room with the ministers, the mothers were ushered in, and the wedding party rustled down the aisle. Marion's 5-year-old sister carefully dropped flower petals along the white pathway. Then Marion entered, nervous and well worth waiting for, Jack's smile told everyone.

"Do you promise . . . ?"

"Yes, I do!"

After prayer, Osgood pronounced the glowing couple man and wife. Since they had never kissed on the lips before, their noses got in the way the first swing. They both awkwardly turned their heads a couple of times before making contact. The more than 400 people present broke out in happy applause.

Rice, balloons, and an old shoe sent them off on a happy honeymoon, which they spent driving back to Washington

State to complete the final three months of Jack's military service. They began and ended every day by worshiping God together. Their love and respect for each other and for God continued to deepen.

Once they had settled in their quarters, Marion received from the local church names of people who needed to be visited. She thoroughly enjoyed the Tacoma church family and associating again with Pastor and Mrs. Osgood. The young couple marked off the days until Jack would be discharged from the military in early January.

"Where do you recommend that I go to college?" he asked Elder Osgood.

"We have some excellent colleges," the older man replied. "My daughters went to Union College in Lincoln, Nebraska, and loved every brick of the place."

So Jack sent in an application to attend second semester at Union College and was accepted. The couple began making plans for a new adventure to begin with Jack's discharge from the military shortly after the first of January.

Late in the afternoon of December 31 Marion stopped behind a car turning left, signaling to make the same turn herself. Another driver approached from behind. Momentarily distracted by her child, she failed to see the two stopped cars. Just as the lead car successfully turned, the young mother's auto crashed full force into Marion's vehicle, catapulting it far down the highway. Cars had no headrests or seat belts in those days, and the impact violently jerked Marion's head forward and backward. Miraculously, though stunned and extremely sore, she could walk, and the car was drivable. The driver of the other car and her children were bruised, but otherwise unhurt.

"I'm so thankful to God for sparing my life," Marion told Jack later when she picked him up at the Air Force base, still trembling. "Of *course*, I want to go on to prayer meeting tonight. God took special care of me today."

The next day she went for X-rays. "Time will heal this injury," the doctor assured her, "but it will be painful for several days, maybe even weeks."

However, the pain from the whiplash in her neck seemed instead to increase with each passing day. She became unable to turn her head from side to side. With months of physical therapy, traction, and heat treatments, she regained some movement, but eventually lost that ability. She bore the intense pain stoically, grateful that the Lord had spared her life.

Jack received his discharge from the military the second week in January 1953, and despite his wife's recent serious injury, the time came to begin the trip to Union College. They finished loading all their belongings into their hastily repaired car, had prayer in the driveway, and headed east toward Nebraska. To save money and time, they drove night and day. The weather grew constantly colder, and before long, it began to snow. Driving in the darkness was nerve-racking, with dropping temperatures and a blinding kaleidoscope of snowflakes peppering the windshield.

As day lightened into early dawn, without warning they suddenly struck a long patch of black ice. Unexpectedly, the car spun completely around, slinging them against each other before the little Plymouth came to a standstill in a field just off the road's shoulder, facing east again.

"While we're stopped, let's read the Morning Watch text and have prayer," Jack suggested weakly, his knees feeling like jelly.

Marion read the day's text, Luke 21:36: "Watch ye therefore, and pray always, that ye may be accounted worthy to escape all these things that shall come to pass . . ."

Amused at the appropriateness of the promise, they again thanked God for His care over their lives. Mercifully, the sun peeked above the horizon and helped make driving a bit easier.

When they arrived in Lincoln, Nebraska, it was extremely cold. Having few resources except $136 a month from the military, Jack saved money by wearing his Air Force uniform to school, stripped of its military insignia. The warm Eisenhower jacket and pants were well made of good material and lasted through his entire college career.

Marion, having learned thriftiness at home, now became more creative with beans, rice, homemade bread, and peanut butter. Even with all the penny-pinching, of course, they still had to find jobs. She discovered that a woman with a college degree in religion did not at the time have a lot of marketable skills. A college counselor suggested, "If you take some summer classes in methods and one in classroom management, you could begin teaching this fall."

"You know, Jack," Marion said, "while we're in a college setting, I'd like to go ahead and get an additional degree in education. Now would be the ideal time to do it." It did not take long, however, to realize that if they were going to survive, Marion would have to quit school and work full-time. A small one-room country school hired her to teach. Jack labored part time on the school farm, then on the grounds crew, and later as a stocker in the neighborhood grocery store while attending classes and studying.

Money was tight, but they had each other. They also had Twirpsie, a canary Marion had been given in Chicago that brought a lot of song and laughter to their home. Jack even taught Twirpsie to do a few tricks. Early each morning the little bird flew out of his cage and landed flapping and singing beautifully on the headboard of their bed. Sometimes he sat on the edge of the newspaper Jack was reading, looking down with his head cocked curiously as if to inquire, "Whatever is so interesting?"

In his eagerness to finish college and begin working for God, Jack took the heaviest class loads possible. Marion became engrossed in teaching her children in the one-room, eight-grade public school in rural Nebraska. It had no indoor plumbing and only a potbellied stove (which she must stoke) for heat. The children, however, were a delight, and Marion loved them all.

In late winter a visit to the doctor confirmed the joyous news. "It looks like you will become parents yourselves this fall!" the doctor said. Marion began to happily stitch and sew tiny little garments whenever she could spare a few minutes.

Then an ominous phone call from her mother followed the good news. "Marion, dear, I'm afraid I have bad news. The doctor tells me I have cancer. I—I don't know how much time I have."

Marion immediately got her schoolwork in order, arranged for another teacher to relieve her, and went to spend two weeks with her mother in Holly, Michigan, where she had recently moved. Mrs. Blasius lived only a few months, and her concerned daughter spent every moment she could with her. They talked hopefully about playing together with the expected baby, but it was not to be. Because the two had been so close, it was especially difficult for Marion when her mother finally died, though she realized it was a blessing that her mother's pain was now over. At least she had been able to be with her at the end. Perhaps the arrival of the new baby would help her through her own grief.

Jack was studying for a Greek exam in the middle of a November night in 1954 when his wife announced, "I think it's time to go!" They rushed to the hospital. It was a difficult delivery that lasted many hours, and Marion, so slight in stature, was over-sedated. Tiny Cheryl Ann screamed a lusty protest at joining the world, indicating that all was well with her. However, when Marion was wheeled out, she looked so deathly pale and still on the white sheets that Jack thought she was dead. He touched her cold hand, and it was alarmingly lifeless. Immediately he put his ear to her mouth to be sure she was breathing and was greatly relieved and thankful to discover she was.

She had to give up her teaching position, and from that point until Jack graduated, kept children in their home (at 10 cents an hour per child) in order to be a full-time mother to

Cheryl Ann. Twirpsie often flew to Marion's shoulder and thoughtfully observed every motherly attention.

Jack was so eager to tell the world of his soon-coming Lord that he could hardly stand to waste a moment of preparation time to get on with that focus of his life. When a two-week vacation approached, he signed up for a two-hour correspondence course. If the vacation would be three weeks, he enrolled for a three-hour course. The Lord blessed his dedication and efforts, and he completed college in two and a half years with straight A's in his major classes and the top score in the senior comprehensive exams. For some reason, however, in 1955 the conferences hired only one or two ministerial students from his entire class. The few openings seemed to be for combination colporteur/pastor or teacher/pastor positions. (It meant that a person would sell books or teach elementary school full-time and pastor on the side while waiting and hoping for a full-time pastoral opening.)

Because of his minor in history, an academy offered Jack a position as a history teacher. As they discussed it, he said with concern, "I'm so certain God called me to the ministry that teaching history doesn't seem to be the direction we should go now. But I also know I need to support my family."

After praying long and intently, both Jack and Marion felt strongly that he should attend the seminary in Washington, D.C., to further prepare himself to serve as a minister. "God will provide," they assured each other.

After graduation in August, they started with 9-month-old Cheryl Ann toward the nation's capital in their jam-packed little Plymouth. Having no air conditioner and pulling a fully loaded trailer with their packed car, it was an extremely difficult trip. Alas, the heat in the car was too much for Twirpsie. He had to be buried before they were out of Nebraska.

Upon arriving in the District of Columbia, they quickly settled into a seminary apartment and discovered, not surprisingly, that finances were a major problem. Actually, Jack had planned to work full-time or more the first quarter in order to get them established and then plow into schoolwork, but a visit to the school business office burst that bubble of hope.

"I'm sorry, but you cannot stay in a school apartment unless you are actually enrolled this quarter," the assistant said firmly.

Jack tried desperately but unsuccessfully to find part-time work. In those days few, if any, students had sponsorships or scholarships. Everyone was pretty much on their own. Finally, through an employment agency, Marion was able to get a teaching job to support them, though the finder's fee consumed their meager savings.

Before classes began each day Jack usually took Cheryl Ann to the baby-sitter (with all the paraphernalia involved), and when classes ended he returned to pick her up. He learned on Fridays (the seminary had no classes then) to be a house-husband, a far more difficult task than he had anticipated. He tried to study while holding or watching the active youngster, washing and hanging out diapers and other clothes, preparing meals, washing dishes, cleaning house, and getting everything ready for Sabbath—it was a lesson in appreciation of a mother's work that he never forgot.

Winter was long and cold that year, and one day after playing outside without her bonnet on, the blond girl became mysteriously ill and listless. Within hours, after refusing food or drink, she developed a dangerously high fever—105°F. They rushed her to Washington Sanitarium and Hospital, and the nurses did all they could, but her tiny veins simply would not accept the IV needle necessary to restore fluids to her dehydrating body. Her little fingers began to turn blue. Helpless and in despair, her parents turned to God.

"Dear Father, please don't let her die! We need a miracle from You," they pleaded with greater urgency than they had ever known possible.

Suddenly, the child's own pediatrician, Dr. Ruth Standard, appeared in the emergency room and said gently to the distraught parents, "I want you to go to the waiting room and pray while I work with Cheryl Ann."

Obediently, they did as they were told, watching in helpless agony as an oxygen tank rolled past them toward their little girl's room. Then the doctor personally administered rectal fluids and oxygen, and the pale, lifeless toddler's vital signs began to stabilize. After an hour and a half, Dr. Standard finally appeared, smiling, at the door of the waiting room. Jack and Marion knew it was good news. "You and your God did a great job," the doctor said. She, too, had been praying as she worked.

The Blancos praised God for answered prayer through the skill of a caring physician. The doctor suggested that Cheryl Ann should have a blood transfusion the next day to further stabilize her. Jack's blood matched his daughter's exactly, and this time, through an artery in her neck, the transfusion was successful, bringing about a dramatic transformation. Her pale cheeks turned pink immediately, and she quickly became her usual inquisitive little self again.

It was hard on the child not to have her mother close at hand during the long days. Once when Jack picked her up at the sitter's, she pointed to a stump in the yard and said pensively, "Dat's where I 'pie' and 'pie' for Mommy and Daddy!" Jack still had an undissolved lump in his throat when he related the incident to his wife.

At the close of the school year the job Jack had applied for finally opened up. The Golden Rule Dairy was closed on Saturdays but delivered milk twice on Fridays. Now at last Marion could stay home with their child as they had planned, and Jack would work full-time to support his family while finishing school. They recognized the job as a special blessing from God.

Every day was exciting for Cheryl Ann, especially now that her mother was home. The toddler's animated curiosity, however, kept her perpetually in trouble. One day an older child showed her a beautiful blue flash bulb. Her tiny fingers captured the treasure, and she immediately bit into the strange "grape." Marion heard the other child saying, "Spit it out! Spit it out!" and went running to the scene. Cheryl Ann looked questioningly up at her mother, smiled—and swallowed. Jack was not yet home, so Marion frantically asked another seminary student to take them to the emergency room.

"What you need to do," the hospital advised Marion, "is to feed the little one all the mashed potatoes she will eat for the next three days. The potatoes will help encase any shards of glass as they pass through."

The doctor also said, "You need to watch for abdominal distention, fever, or blood in the stool. Any of these symptoms could indicate surgery. If you don't see any evidence of those things, then you'll know everything is going to be OK."

Jack's new job, delivering milk, accommodated his school schedule. Obviously, in order for customers to have their milk before breakfast, he had to work the route early in the morning—beginning no later than 2:00 a.m. Quickly Jack figured out that if he ran from the truck to each of his hundred customers, he could complete his route in time to dash home, shave, shower, and gulp down a quick breakfast before arriving, breathless, at his 8:00 a.m. classes. Driving the truck standing up, he memorized each customer's order. Then he would grab up to four quarts of bottled milk (two in each hand) and sprint to the front or back of the house as needed, snatch up the empty glass bottles waiting on the porch, and run back to the truck. Any time a customer had a special order he would have to go back and forth again and then remember to write it down in the log book before speeding on to the next house.

One evening he was late getting to bed, and 1:30 came especially early. Nevertheless, he dressed quickly, drove to the dairy, and hurriedly loaded the truck with scores of cases of milk and sped off into the night. Near the end of his frenzied run through the last sleepy neighborhood, he grabbed one family's usual order of two quarts of milk in one hand and bounded out of the truck, loping across the front lawn as he had always done.

But the owners, having re-seeded bare spots in the grass, had driven stakes with wire pulled taut between them in various areas. They had tied little flags on the wires in hopes of discouraging neighbor children from playing there until the new grass came up. But in the darkness Jack did not see the wire or the strips of cloth, and his shoes caught under a wire just before he reached the sidewalk. With feet entangled and body still on a forward course, he plunged to the ground, smashing the bottles of milk on the concrete and gouging his hand in the broken glass. Because everything hit the cement at once, the crash sounded like an explosion. He lay there a moment, afraid he had awakened the neighborhood and wondering if he would lose his customers.

However, no angry calls rang out and no one came, so he quickly pulled himself up and hurried back to the truck. There he found his flashlight, a container for the broken glass, and some rags to mop up the milk. As he hurriedly blotted the sidewalk, he noticed that the spilled milk was turning red. Sure enough, he had a deep gash in his left hand. After tying a clean rag around his hand to slow the bleeding, he finished mopping up the milk, carefully picking up all the broken glass he could see. Finding an outside faucet, he hosed the sidewalk clean, then hurriedly delivered the family's milk order. Since the cut was so deep and was still bleeding profusely, he decided to go to the hospital for stitches. He sped back to the dairy, but only one person was there.

"Al, is there any way you could finish my run for me? I just got a nasty cut." Jack held up his bloody hand.

"Boy, Jack, that *is* bad," Al acknowledged sympathetically, "but I just started the milking machinery, and there's no way I can leave right now. Someone else should be here within an hour. Why don't you sit down and rest till it stops bleeding?"

Jack decided his job was too valuable to risk losing customers by not leaving milk for them on time. With a prayer on his lips that he would not pass out from losing so much blood, he climbed back into the truck and returned to the neighborhood to finish his route. One rag after another became soaked in red, so when he ran out of clean ones, he simply let blood accumulate in the cupped palm of his right hand and emptied it on the street as he drove along. (No one was concerned about blood-borne pathogens back then.)

Returning to the dairy, he unloaded the truck as quickly as possible with one hand, then jumped into his car and drove to the emergency room. There they put numerous stitches in his hand. The young physician remarked, "That cut was within a hair breadth of severing both your artery and tendon."

After a long gulp of orange juice and a brief rest in the emergency room, he drove home, showered, shaved, ate on the run—and arrived at his first-period class with seconds to spare.

CHAPTER EIGHTEEN

Pastor Blanco

The seminary assigned all students as pastoral assistants to various churches in the area. Jack had the Vienna, Virginia, church. Now weekends became even busier than other days of the week. The church was in the midst of a building campaign. The congregation had to sell the old structure and plan and build a new facility, with a church school to be constructed first. The pastor, of course, expected his assistant to set a sacrificial example in giving, regardless of school bills or family responsibilities. A hundred dollars was a lot of money back in the 50s, especially for a student family with one income and almost four mouths to feed, but Jack and Marion figured, "Jesus gave His life for us, and whatever we can do for Him, we will." So together they gave from the meager amount they had, and the Lord blessed them in many other ways, not at all to their surprise.

One January 1958 evening as Jack was studying for a Hebrew exam, Marion said, "I think we'd better get to the hospital—quick!" This time the birthing process went fast, and Stephen was born. Life became busier and noisier at home, but Jack was not able to be at home with his family very much. Her grandchildren seemed to dissipate Katie Blanco's prejudices toward her son's religion, and she became more warm and loving toward the entire family.

Jack had already received his Master of Arts in religion and was in the last quarter toward his Master of Divinity degree (the final degree expected of prospective pastors) when the big question became "Where—or *will*—I go to work?" Conference presidents came to the campus and began to interview. Some students were chosen and some, equally qualified, were not.

"Honey, let's just pray earnestly about it," he told his wife confidently. "I believe the Lord called me to the ministry. He will open the way in His own time. We'll trust Him."

Dr. Melvin Eckenroth, a former professor at the seminary, had recently become president of the New Jersey Conference. As graduation approached, Jack received a telephone call from him. "We have an opening for an energetic young minister with a passion for evangelism," his former teacher said. "I immediately thought of you. Are you interested?"

So in 1958 they again packed the Blanco car, this time including all the trappings for a 3-year-old daughter and an 8-month-old son, and headed for Newark.

"Jack," Elder Eckenroth said, "we would like you to go to the Morristown/Rockaway district to help the pastor start a church. There is no Seventh-day Adventist church in Morristown, but there are a few believers. I plan to come and hold evangelistic meetings myself, and you and the pastor can prepare the way and then help me with the series."

The family found a small apartment on a busy highway and hurriedly moved in. Jack immediately went to work, and Marion had to handle the details of establishing their home.

Little Stephen was not to be outdone by Cheryl Ann's incident with the flash bulb. He managed to extract his comb from his diaper bag, and before his mother knew it, chewed off a mouthful of plastic teeth. When she checked on him in the midst of preparing lunch, the comb's teeth were missing. Her fingers desperately probed his mouth, but Stephen only laughed. Another rush to the hospital. This time the doctor did not feel it was serious. Instead, she said, "There really shouldn't be a problem. The plastic teeth will pretty well dissolve and digest when they reach the stomach acids. But, again, you need to watch for blood in the stool and all the other things."

Evangelistic meetings convened in a rented hall. Jack conducted the music, and Marion helped with the children's meetings and did black-light chalk drawings to go with the closing appeal song. The series resulted in about 35 baptisms and a small church organized. First with the pastor, and later on his own, Jack nurtured that little congregation.

In spite of strong prejudice against Seventh-day Adventists in the area, the congregation began to enlarge, and before long their rented hall became too small. They started looking for a church building to rent. However, no church was willing to rent to the Adventists. A prominent pastor in the area had spoken vehemently against them, vowing to drive them out of town. The congregation offered fervent prayers for divine direction, and when God's answer became apparent, it seemed too good to be true.

"I'll sell the church seven acres just outside the city limits for exactly what I paid for it years ago," a member pledged, and it was a most reasonable price. Soon they had it paid for, and the little Morristown group wondered what to do next. By now the little hall in which they continued to meet had standing room only.

"I'll lend the church enough money to build a large parsonage with room in the basement for us to meet," another member offered. They drew up plans to include a large lower level open all along the back side of the house that would seat 144 people and would also contain a kitchen and a Dorcas room. Jack and his family would live upstairs, and their rent would pay the mortgage. The home had four large bedrooms upstairs, but the family could get by with using only two of them plus a study that they converted into a primary/junior classroom on Sabbaths. The other room became a cradle roll/kindergarten room, with Marion in charge. Of course, the church had no budget for Sabbath school supplies, so she made her own every week. Jack, in addition to his pastoral duties, also served as caretaker of the property.

As the construction crew excavated for the house, it also dug a pond that was fed and kept fresh by a stream on the property, furnishing an ideal place for the frequent baptisms. As far as convenience, the setup might not necessarily be what Jack and Marion would have chosen, but it was a wonderful place for children to roam and play. And now the city had an established congregation where previously there had been none. The couple felt that they could tolerate a little inconvenience in light of God's obvious leading. The members seemed to love their young pastor and his family.

No sooner was the Morristown congregation established than Jack saw other needs nearby. The next county had no Seventh-day Adventist church, so he began a branch Sabbath school in Somerville that soon grew into a small congregation. He felt God impressed him to develop Bible study interests in the tiny town of Flemington. Soon he was pastoring a three-church district, each one needing attention. It meant preaching at three churches each Sabbath: one at 9:30, one at 11:00, and the last one at 2:30. The family often took a lunch and accompanied him to the afternoon service, singing, "We are a missionary band . . . doing all we can." The children, quite naturally, were not always enthusiastic about sitting through two services and waiting—*always* waiting, it seemed—for Daddy. But they enjoyed their own Sabbath school while their father was at one of the other services. As for Jack, it was the joy of his life to see men, women, and children give their hearts to Jesus Christ, and to watch the flame of the Holy Spirit rekindled in the lives of those who were already Christians.

By now Cheryl Ann was 6 years old and ready for school, but there was no church school nor enough children to support one. "Mother, I wish I had some friends to play with," she pined day after day. Jack and Marion finally decided to enroll her in the first grade of public school. She loved it. When school was out, she could hardly wait to get home and teach 3-year-old Stephen what she had learned. He, on the other hand, was not quite so willing for big sister to wreck his carefree day and try to force him to sit still. Both children soon became frustrated. "But Daddy, he doesn't even *want* to learn—he wants to be *ignorant* all his life."

Her brother protested, "I don't *wanna* play school—I just wanna go outside and ride my trike."

Cheryl Ann became distressed over the length of her name. "Mother, I'm still writing my name when everyone else is finished. I think I'll go by Cheri from now on," she asserted. Her interest in school somewhat diminished later in the year when the teacher solemnly announced, "The sun is gradually burning itself out. Eventually, the earth will get cold and freeze over, and there will be another ice age." The girl came home crying over the imminent fate of the earth.

"Cheri, who made the sun?" her father asked, taking her onto his lap to comfort her.

"God did," she sniffled.

"Well, don't you think that if God can make a sun, He can keep it burning? Maybe not everyone understands that." The answer seemed to satisfy her.

The children spent many long hours waiting for their father to finish talking to people after church, though they sensed the important role that he played in so many parishioners' lives. Years later they both agreed that in their home they had never heard others spoken of in any way that could be construed as gossip or criticism, a kindness they discovered to be rare in others.

But with their father gone so much and their mother often involved in helping at the church or substitute teaching, Cheri and Stephen decided what they really needed was a dog. It was a serious matter that called for serious prayer. At worship and bedtime they prayed that God would send them a dog of their very own. Their parents reminded them that dogs were expensive to buy and maintain.

Shortly after beginning their prayer request, they awoke one morning to find a black Belgian shepherd lying sleepily on the parsonage steps. Since they lived out in the country, their parents were at a loss to know where it had come from. But the children believed that they knew. It was just hard to believe that He had answered them so quickly.

Later that day the phone rang. An unfamiliar voice asked, "Did you find a black dog in your yard?"

"Yes." Steve's heart sank.

"Well, his name is Blackie, and you can have him." *Click.*

That was all they ever knew about where the dog came from, but never was a dog more loved. And they remembered to thank the One who had sent him.

Just as the growing Morristown congregation was making plans to build a church sanctuary, the conference moved Jack to Woodbury, in the southern part of the state near Philadelphia where a new church and school were almost completed. His assignment was simple—double the membership from 100 to 200.

The church scheduled the first series of evangelistic meetings to start in February, the only time Roger Holley and his evangelistic team were free to come. Elder Holley would begin his meetings on Sunday evening and continue them nightly for three weeks with two meetings held on Sabbath.

The congregation mailed out handbills, and members invited as many people as they could personally contact. Then Saturday night it began to snow. It blew down from the north and increased in intensity every hour—a large and totally unexpected snowstorm. By Sunday morning the snow had almost stopped, but the nearly impassable roads had almost no traffic. Even if people could get there, where would they park? Three feet of snow covered the church parking lot. Pastor Holley and Jack spent most of the day shoveling the parking area, determined to go ahead with the opening meeting that night, no matter what.

Sure enough, when evening came, only a handful of church members showed up, plus one non-Adventist family of five who had slowly and carefully driven in from 20 miles away. The next day the snow began to melt, and attendance quickly picked up until the church had standing room only. The family of five came faithfully every night and were the first to be baptized. The meetings produced 60 baptisms and stirred up so many additional interests that Jack planned a second series for the following year.

It was a lot of hard work, with Jack heavily involved in visitation and Bible studies. It seemed that almost every member of the church participated. "They don't know it, but we're going to love these people right into the church!" one person said.

During this very busy time of their lives Jack decided to take advantage of living fairly close to Princeton Theological Seminary. He enrolled in "Minister's Monday," an opportunity for local pastors to come in for classes. Every Monday he got up early and drove to Princeton, taking classes in church history, focusing on church/state issues.

Marion caught the learning fever also, and since they were near Glassboro State Teachers' College, she decided to complete her master's degree in teaching. However, just before school was to start that fall, one of the church school teachers suddenly resigned and the conference could not find another one anywhere. The conference (and Jack) persuaded Marion to help out, thus postponing again her desire to further her own education.

When the time came for the second series of meetings to begin in Woodbury, Elder Holley once again served as speaker, and his new singing evangelist was young Robert Folkenberg (who became General Conference president in 1990), together with his wife and newborn son, also named Robert. With another successful campaign Jack's second year there, the membership more than doubled. This led the conference to ask him to help other churches in his area to adopt similar programs. Later he received a phone call from the New Jersey Conference office.

"Would you be interested in becoming our conference evangelist? We are trying to work out a budget right now for just such a position."

"Wow, I'd like to think and pray about that," Jack replied.

That evening Marion didn't tell him about the letter that had come in the mail earlier that day. Instead, she asked, "If you got a call to go to Africa as a missionary, would you go?"

"I would go tomorrow," Jack replied confidently.

"Well, here, read this." She handed him the official letter.

He could hardly believe what he was reading. The letter with the General Conference return address inquired if he would be interested in going to Solusi College in Africa to help train young men in evangelism.

How could they decide which call was from God? Should they take their children to Africa? What about the offer to do evangelism right here? What did God want them to do? Prayer didn't seem to give them a direct answer. Instead, the Lord seemed to nudge first one direction, then the other. Back and forth it went, and the more counsel they sought, the more uncertain they felt. It became a game with the children. "Daddy," they teased, "is this the day we're going to Africa, or is this the day we're staying here?"

Finally, Jack drove alone to Washington, D.C., to the Columbia Union office and talked with Elder Neal Wilson, the union president. His advice helped solve the dilemma: "If you have no reason not to go overseas, you need to go."

That seemed to make sense. So the family accepted the offer in Africa. Marion knew it would put an end to her educational plans, but she was a bit unsure of her role. "What will I be expected to do?" she asked the General Conference representative.

His reply relieved her anxiety. "Just look after the health and welfare of your family," he said reassuringly.

Young Cheri especially felt constrictions from the near-poverty level income her minister father received at the time. She fought the envious feelings she had when other children came to school with new boxes of crayons—a luxury she would not even ask for. Perhaps going to Africa would, she thought, give her the same noble commitment to God and church that her father had.

Steve's 7-year-old imagination conjured up ideas of living in the jungle with cannibals, fighting off lions, and sleeping with snakes. He detected that even his mother harbored some anticipation along with the excitement of venturing into the unknown.

About that time Elder Robert Pierson, the Trans-Africa Division president, came to the U.S.A. on furlough and advised Jack, "You really ought to finish your Princeton degree before going overseas if at all possible." Fortunately, the professors at Princeton cooperated. Shortly before Jack completed his master's degree in theology (a year beyond the Master of Divinity degree he had earned at the seminary), the packing began in earnest.

Ten years in the ministry with several moves had already kept their possessions to a minimum, but even so, they had to sell carefully acquired treasures or store them with willing church members. They signed the little house they had recently purchased with a GI loan over to the conference as a gift, to be used as a parsonage. They would be in Africa for five long years, so surely they would not need it again. Christ would probably come before then. Even if He didn't, they did not want the responsibility of a house hanging over them while living so many thousands of miles away.

It took careful planning to arrange to be at the graduation ceremonies at Princeton just before leaving for New York and ultimately Africa. And they felt mixed emotions—heavy hearts at leaving loves ones, yet pleasure at being called to mission service. The little family said a tearful goodbye to the Woodbury congregation they loved, goodbye to family (Katie and Lee Blanco came to the Princeton graduation, sad to see them, yet fiercely proud of her son), and goodbye to friends. Several church members from Woodbury accompanied them to Princeton, and then, joined by Morristown friends, to New York

City. A wealthy member took the entire family and their guests out to eat in a restaurant as a farewell gesture and insisted on having young Steve sit next to her. The children were almost as excited over this, their first real restaurant experience, as they were about their imminent trip halfway around the world.

They all boarded the ship together, and one of their friends gave them a package with a gift to be opened each day of their voyage. Then, with tears and a final parting prayer, Jack, Marion, 10-year-old Cheri, and 7-year-old Steve waved from the deck as their friends departed. At midnight the ship pulled anchor, and they departed for South Africa.

Well, at least they would have time to relax on the 20-day ocean voyage. After so many months of intense activity, the family really looked forward to that.

Chapter Nineteen

Africa

After they began to wind down from the excitement, Jack showed the children around the big ship. "When I was about your age, my mother took me on my first trip across the ocean to visit my grandparents in Germany," he told them.

As they walked and talked, he couldn't help noticing how old the freighter appeared to be and how much obvious maintenance work it required. For the sake of the ship, he secretly hoped the crew would not delay the work much longer.

But he should not have worried. At 6:00 the next morning the family awoke to the sound of jackhammers and riveting guns—a racket that continued daily from daybreak till dark until they docked in Cape Town almost three weeks later. So much for their restful cruise!

Being a freighter, the ship carried few passengers. The captain, however, was most gracious, and invited all guests to eat with him in the small lounge reserved for such purposes. The cook was especially solicitous. "Your whole family is vegetarian? We will do our best to care for your needs. What do you like?"

At least twice a week the captain showed slides or home movies about his world travels. Sometimes he entertained his guests with games. A diminutive Catholic nun and medical doctor was also a passenger on the freighter. She was headed to central Africa to open a clinic in the bush country, and the Blancos felt an immediate kinship with her.

Once a week everyone on board had to participate in rescue drills during which large lifeboats, one on each side, were alternately lowered into the water. At that time everyone had to wear life vests, but only the crew had to actually get into the lifeboats and be lowered overboard.

"Steve and Cheri," the cook called one day as they finished their meal, "let's do something special today. How would you like to write out some messages on a piece of paper? We'll stuff them into empty bottles, seal them, and then toss the bottles overboard. No telling who will find them."

The first bottle shattered when it hit the water, but the others bobbed away, and the children vividly imagined where the bottles would land and who would find their messages.

The ship and its many crannies fascinated Steve. About 10 feet above the deck, protruding metal rods were spaced close enough together to tempt any youngster to swing like a monkey from one to the next, and Steve enjoyed doing just that. One day as he swung along he didn't notice the vessel rising on a large ocean swell. While he was in midair swinging to the next rod, the ship rolled, and suddenly he had nothing to grab. He plummeted facedown against the hard wooden deck, smashing his nose and momentarily knocking the breath out of him. A quick and tearful visit to the Catholic doctor confirmed that, though bloody and bruised, his nose was not broken, nor did he have a concussion.

Far out into the ocean, when the captain was sure there were no other ships in the vicinity, he shot some outdated flares high into the air, providing a little fireworks display. Some days huge swells rolled in from nearby storms. During those times the ship rode high on the mighty waves, then plunged to the base of the swells, rolling precariously from side to side and causing the horizon to alternate between the floor and ceiling of the dining room window. At those times they were all seasick, especially Marion and Cheri. It made them all grateful for calm seas. They docked briefly at such places as St. Helena island, where Napoleon had spent his final years. There Steve and Cheri watched in fascination as the crew opened the cargo bay and loaded and unloaded huge crates and other goods. At the crystal-clear water's edge schools of fish swept by. The crew did not allow anyone off the ship, but the sailors delighted the children and other passengers by reaching into the water and catching some of the fish with their bare hands.

At one island off the coast of western Africa where a diamond mine had recently shut down, Steve spotted the afternoon sun glinting off what, to him, appeared to be thousands of diamonds just lying on the surface.

"Dad, why can't we just go over there and pick up a few handfuls? Then we wouldn't need to worry about going to Africa and working in the middle of the jungle."

"Well, Steve," his father answered gently, "for one thing, I don't really think those are diamonds lying on the surface of the ground. But even if they were, we've got a much more important work to do. God didn't put us here to see how rich we can get. Someday we'll walk on streets paved with gold. Maybe He will use us here to help others know how much He loves them so they can be in heaven too."

At last, one bright and beautiful Thursday, they approached the majestic mountains and skyline of Cape Town. As they prepared to disembark, they asked the Catholic nun, "Will someone be meeting you to help you reach your destination?"

"No, I don't expect anyone to be here," she replied. "I'm on my own now and will head toward central Africa immediately."

As Jack, Marion, and the children watched the crates with their goods being unloaded to go by train 1,500 miles north to Rhodesia (now Zimbabwe), they felt grateful for their church family which, even here in Africa, looked after its own. Perhaps their sacrifice was not so great after all.

"Welcome to Africa!" their host said enthusiastically. "I'm

going to handle all the necessary paperwork here. Let's get your things, and we'll hire a cab to take you to your hotel. You might want to go sightseeing tomorrow, but we hope you'll join us for Sabbath dinner. It will probably be Monday before your goods will be checked through customs, so maybe you'll have a chance to look around a bit." He suggested some interesting places to visit.

The next day they picked up the square-back Volkswagen that Jack had ordered from Germany and had come in on another ship. He had requested that the steering wheel be on the right, since cars drove on the left in Africa. But perhaps because the order came from the United States, the VW arrived with the steering wheel on the left. So for the next five years in Africa, Jack drove on the left with the steering wheel on the left. Marion decided to wait until their return to the United States to drive again.

They spent Sabbath with their new friend and his family, who showed them around Cape Town. On Sunday the children enjoyed a cable car ride to the top of Table Mountain, so named because the top of the mountain was flat, and clouds often hung over it, making it look like a table covered with a cloth. The culture in Africa was quite different with a lot to get used to in a short time. Some things they found difficult to accept, such as the way Whites treated people with dark-colored skin.

On Monday the Blancos climbed into their new VW and started on the 1,500-mile trip up through South Africa, pausing at Johannesburg, Pretoria, and various church institutions along the way. Finally they crossed the border into Rhodesia and headed for Bulawayo, then out toward Solusi Mission. A short distance out of town the paved road ended, and the next 30 miles of dirt road seemed to be a washboard determined to shake the little VW apart. The slower Jack drove, the more the car shook. (Later, he learned that the way to drive on such a dirt road is to drive fast and "fly" over the top of it all.)

At Solusi Mission the staff welcomed them and showed

them their quarters, a simple house built on a cement slab with a tin roof. Behind the house stood a small corncob-burning stove used to heat the 44-gallon drum of water that sat on the roof. Inside was a living room, dining room, kitchen, and three bedrooms. A small three-sided garage for their VW sat on one side of the house. On the other side was a little vegetable garden and fruit orchard. Their home, of course, had no air conditioning or heat, but then, neither did anyone else's. Jack pronounced it comfortable and adequate.

The college president and his wife invited the Blancos over for their first few meals and helped them get acquainted with the mission, its facilities, what items were available there, and what had to be secured in town 30 miles away. "Most missionary families go to town weekly to get what they need," the president's wife said.

The other missionaries had come not only from the United States, but also from England, Australia, New Zealand, South Africa, and even from Rhodesia itself. Besides the college campus, the station included a large secondary and elementary school, plus a school farm.

"Solusi College is 4,000 feet above sea level, and the temperature here is perfect most of the time—sometimes into the 40s at night," the president told them. "If you get too warm during the day, just go stand under a tree, and the breeze will cool you off."

Every day dawned bright and beautiful, with fluffy white clouds peppering the azure sky. Sabbaths often found the 20 or so missionaries enjoying a potluck dinner at a nearby kopje (a large pile of boulders, often with caves and/or animal life). Not far away was a game park where the family enjoyed seeing African animals in their natural habitat. It was better than any zoo.

Soon after their arrival the mission began rationing water. A severe drought had struck the entire country, and each person could use only so much water a day. Before long the water from their pipes came out muddy and brown-colored. They bathed and washed their clothes in it because it was all they had. Water for drinking and cooking came from a large cistern that still held a small supply of last year's rain. Soon the drought became so intense that desperate villagers started coming to the mission for food. Infants and young cattle were dying all around them.

"We must begin a feeding program," Robert Pierson, the division president, alerted the other missionaries. "Sudza [cornmeal] once a day will help keep many people alive. We cannot be called Christ's servants if we do not do Christ's work."

The food lines stretched endlessly as people lined up to be served. Pierson and his wife always helped serve the meals, along with the other missionaries. The nearby Salvation Army mission had to close because of the severe drought. At the Adventist mission prayer ascended daily for water. Weeks passed. It became obvious that their mission station would have to close soon also. Since Jack was also serving as church pastor at the time, he called for the entire mission compound to hold a prayer vigil the next Friday night. Then on Sabbath a special prayer meeting convened immediately after the brief preaching service.

"We are going to pray for rain and pour out our hearts to our merciful Father," Pierson announced. "Perhaps He will see fit to send us a blessing."

Almost everyone in the congregation remained to participate. About 1:00 p.m. Jack and Marion went home to care for their family and the woman missionary they had invited to lunch.

As they sat down to eat, Jack again implored God for a miracle. "Dear Father, we have nothing but what came from Your hand, and we are grateful for all Your mercies. But we have such a need here for water. We are asking You for a miracle because our human wisdom tells us it's impossible for this mission to remain open. We commit everything into Your hands, recognizing there's no better place for our trust to be. Please help us where our faith is weak. Thank You for Your abundant mercies and for our food today—in Jesus' holy name. Amen."

The meal conversation was solemn and their hearts heavy about the mission's uncertain future. Even the children were unusually quiet. "It's so long past the rainy season now, there certainly doesn't seem to be much hope, does there?" their guest remarked.

"I wonder how God will answer the prayers of these dear people?" Marion mused aloud.

"The missionaries, of course, can go home. But what will happen to the nationals?" Jack questioned. "I feel guilty eating this good meal."

So intensely did they discuss the problem that they did not notice that the room was growing dark.

"Dad, look at the sky!" Steve interrupted. Through the window they could see boiling dark clouds rapidly blackening the sky. Suddenly, without thunder or lightning, a torrential rain burst from the heavens, seeming to unburden a heavy pent-up load. It sounded like a thunderous waterfall beating against the tin roof. Within minutes an inch of water covered the living room floor. Jumping from their unfinished meal, everyone rushed to stuff rags around the front door in an effort to keep more water from coming in. Then in about an hour, just as suddenly as it had begun, the rain stopped.

Later that afternoon they discovered that it had rained only on the mission property, about 8,000 acres. Everywhere else was still dry. Steve and Jack raced down to the mission dam to look at the depth marker. Remarkably, 22 feet of water now stood in the large pond that had been virtually empty. Some water actually overflowed the dam, and the delighted children waded and splashed through it. The downpour drew even more villagers to the mission, and its message seemed to make an even greater impact on the local people. The rain was so obviously God's doing, who could question it?

Cheri and Steve attended the missionary children's one-room grade school. He took the government correspondence course with the other children, while she did her American home study correspondence course from Salisbury. The adjustment to the British system was not easy, but they did remarkably well, thanks to an understanding teacher. The entire family found the British view of the Revolutionary War in the textbooks quite interesting. Later, the teacher retired, and the mission asked Marion to teach, which she did.

School got out early every afternoon, giving Steve and the other boys lots of time to play in the wild bush and wide-open spaces. Friendly nationals taught them some of the African survival techniques, such as how to track animals, hunt, fish, and trap game. The Africans also taught the boys to approach a kopje from downwind in order to smell for a leopard before approaching. Because leopards were not clean in their hunting and feeding habits (unlike other members of the cat family), they had a fairly strong odor, and you could usually detect them before you could see them. Numerous antelope, such as kudu or springbok, monkeys, hyenas, and wild boars or warthogs roamed the bush.

Having shown an early interest in music, Cheri began piano lessons shortly after their arrival and was soon playing for Sabbath school. They planned their trips to Bulawayo so she could take lessons at the Royal Academy of Music while they ran errands, and before long, she was playing the pump organ for junior Sabbath school. Always fond of animals, Steve cared for their milk cow. When Lucky produced a calf, he hand-fed it from a pail, and the calf became so attached to him that the family often referred to it as Steve's shadow. It followed him to school (or anywhere else) and patiently waited until he reappeared so it could accompany him home. Steve used his pet chameleon (which had full run of the house) to kill flies. He would hold Cami with its head aimed at a fly, and *snap!* the fly would disappear with a rapid flick of the lizard's long tongue. Faithful Inky, the dog, and mischievous Minnah, the monkey, kept the family laughing at their many antics. In the morning when the monkey was cold, she would crawl up inside Cheri's sweater and stick her head out the neck.

Minnah was Cheri's special pet, obtained from the animal shelter in Bulawayo. She was extremely active, even for a monkey, and when they picked her up, they wondered about the 30-mile trip home in the car. The SPCA put her in a cardboard carton that Jack placed between the children on the back seat of the car. At first she was quiet, but soon a dark little hand reached out of the opening on top of the box. Suddenly, she pulled down both flaps, then was everywhere in the car at once. To quiet her, Marion pulled a ripe banana from under the seat. Minnah grabbed it, but instead of peeling it as monkeys do in pictures, she bit it in the middle, squashed it with her hands, and rudely stuffed the insides into her mouth. Then, seemingly in the interest of hygiene, she thoroughly wiped her hands all over Marion's good coat.

Jack taught college classes for ministerial students who came from across the division that stretched from Kenya to Cape Town. Some were quite young, just out of secondary school; others were much older and had served as evangelists, pastors, or even at the conference departmental level. The church had to upgrade the national leaders and future ministers as quickly as possible. At the end of each school year Jack would take a dozen or more students to a distant city to hold an evangelistic series. They would be gone for at least eight weeks. Each series produced a number of fascinating stories.

One such incident occurred in Lusaka, the capital of Zambia, shortly after the then-White government of Rhodesia had declared its independence from Britain. The African government of Zambia, together with Britain, had opposed such a move. Tension from threats of war between Zambia and Rhodesia filled the air. God had blessed the meetings in Lusaka with about a hundred baptisms, and after eight intense weeks, Jack was eager to get home. Warren Hewes, the publishing secretary, had just finished his appointments also, so they decided to drive several hundred miles during the night so they could reach home by morning.

After sundown they loaded Jack's car, checked to be sure all the students had train tickets home, and then started on their way. Just outside the city the street lights ended and the road narrowed to one lane for nearly the entire journey. Suddenly, out of the dense blackness, a huge spotlight shone into their eyes, nearly blinding them. They came to a screeching halt. As their eyes adjusted to the bright light, they recognized it as a roadblock with a group of Zambian soldiers on alert, looking for infiltrators. Here they were, two White men, returning to Rhodesia, the rebel government next door.

A soldier staggered up to the car, and Hewes rolled down the window. The stench of alcohol told them that the soldier was drunk. He pushed his automatic assault rifle past Hewes and pointed it directly at Jack with his finger on the trigger.

"Where you go?" he demanded with a rude belch.

Jack never remembered praying so hard in all his life. The slightest movement, the soldier losing his balance or stumbling on a rock, would mean Blanco's death. The sentry could hardly speak English, but after a lengthy questioning, they finally convinced him that the two men were missionaries. Slowly he withdrew his weapon from inside the car, stepped back, and waved for them to go. Soaking with nervous perspiration, Jack started the car and drove slowly past the check point, continuing to creep along until they were out of rifle range. Then with a continuous prayer of thanksgiving he literally flew home. He was quite wide awake the rest of that trip and discovered that a VW could reach extreme speeds, even on one-lane dirt roads.

The Matopas game reserve was the perfect spot for a family mini-vacation. Though it had no fences around it, the large tract of land designated as a reserve prohibited hunters and poachers, but people in vehicles could enter at their own risk. One day the family came upon two rhinos grazing about 50 yards off the road. Marion was excitedly taking pictures as Jack inched closer and turned the engine off so as not to disturb them. Suddenly one of the rhinos must have caught a scent, human or gasoline, that it didn't like. Turning, it lowered its head and started to run toward the Blanco vehicle. Jack frantically attempted to start the engine. Marion began to panic and screamed, "Jack! Jack! This thing is coming right at us!"

Steve and Cheri froze with fright in the back seat. Not only was the 7,000-pound behemoth charging at great speed toward their thin-skinned VW, but it was the first time they had ever heard their mother scream. Death must be imminent. They wondered why the car wasn't moving. It seemed an eternity—with the rhino closing the distance rapidly—before finally the car engine fired, the clutch caught, and the little car lurched and jerked its occupants out of the path of the thundering beast.

Chapter Twenty

Miracle in Salisbury

Because the little church in Salisbury, Rhodesia, was too small to hold evangelistic meetings, the congregation requested permission to rent a hall. The person in charge said, "I'm sorry, but we can't rent to you. There are too many religious organizations full of undercover political activists. If we rent to the Adventists, we'd have to rent to all the others as well." The authorities also denied them permission to set up a tent or to hold meetings out-of-doors. Ultimately, the congregation had no choice but to hold the meetings in the little church building.

However, interest was so great that soon the evangelists had to hold two sessions a night, then three, and finally four. The first meeting began at 4:00 p.m.; then 5:00; next 6:00; finally 7:00. This went on every night for three weeks. It was almost too much for Jack. He felt he never fully recovered from the effects of that series of meetings. But how could anyone turn away all the people standing at the windows, waiting to learn of God's love?

Before the meetings began, church members visited every former church member in the area and invited them to the meetings. Jack and his assigned student intern knocked on the door of one such family who had formerly attended church, the Jefferies. In that area the little cement block houses had only a living room and a bedroom—everything else, such as cooking, washing, toiletries, took place outside. A teenage girl answered the door, her two younger sisters in her shadow. She spoke

English fairly well, and after the men introduced themselves, she invited them in. After a bit of small talk, Jack asked, "Would we be able to talk with one of your parents?"

"Father was not able to find work near home," the girl answered, "so he had to move to another town. Even there, the only job he could get involved working on Sabbath." Almost apologetically, she added, "And Mum is very sick in the bedroom."

"Oh, I'm sorry." After visiting briefly with the girls and inviting them to the meetings, he asked, "Do you think your mother would like to come to the living room for us to pray for her? If she doesn't feel up to coming out, we'll still pray for her."

The daughter went in to ask her mother. Shortly, the mother shuffled into the living room, holding her hands out in front of her. Jack would never forget the sight. She had huge red ulcerated sores in the palms of her hands, and her face registered extreme pain. As she gingerly sat down, Jack asked sympathetically, "What happened?"

"Mum has these ulcerated sores also on the soles of her feet, so she cannot walk to church like she used to," the girl explained. "It all started about five years ago when the palms of her hands started to itch. In a few days, blisters formed and filled with liquid. After a few more days the blisters broke open and began to heal, but before they could completely heal, the itching started again, and the process has repeated itself every seven to nine days. Over the years the sores and wounds have just gotten bigger and bigger." She added, "It's the same with her feet."

The mother seemed to understand English but could not speak it, so whenever Jack asked a question, the daughter answered.

"Would you be willing to show me her feet?" Jack asked. The woman revealed the soles of her feet, which looked at least as bad as her hands, if not worse. "Has your mum seen a doctor about this?"

"Yes, but no one has been able to help her, not even the

mission doctor." While the daughter talked, Jack noticed a black string around one of the woman's wrists, indicating that she was either planning to see a witch doctor or already had done so.

The daughter also indicated that her mother could not read. Jack reflected on the difficulties of studying the Bible with such an individual. He knew from experience that an illiterate person must have implicit trust in a minister before he or she will believe, for the individual has no way to check to see if what is being read is true or not.

So for his first visit, Jack simply asked if they could have prayer with the family. He prayed specifically for the mother and reminded her that Jesus loved her. As he and his visitation partner left, the daughter accompanied them to the front gate. The men again invited the daughters to attend the meetings, and they promised they would come.

Then the daughter said, "Mum asked if you would come back tomorrow and pray for her again. Would you be able to do that?"

"Of course," Jack promised. "We'll come back about 9:00 tomorrow morning."

When they arrived the next day, the woman and her daughters were waiting. They talked about her problem, then Jack read a passage from the Bible. Before praying, he asked, "Mum, do you believe that Jesus loves you?"

Her gaze dropped to the floor and she made no response. So the two men prayed and left without pressing the matter and promised to return the next day at the same time. This continued for a couple days, with the daughters attending the meeting each evening. Jack was concerned that if the woman did not believe Jesus loved her, how could she believe He could heal her? Each time they visited, they read Scripture passages and had prayer. One day Jack asked again, "Mum, do you believe that Jesus loves you?" She ever so slightly nodded her head.

The visits continued in much the same way for a few more days. Then the evangelists asked, "Mum, do you believe that Jesus can heal you?"

Again, her gaze dropped and she did not respond. A few days later when Jack asked the same question, she gave another slight nod.

As they left, he suggested, "Since you believe that Jesus loves you and can heal you, you probably won't need that black string around your wrist, will you?" He knew that if he specifically asked her to take it off, she would have done so out of courtesy to him, so he merely made the suggestion and left. The next morning he noticed that the black string had disappeared.

Jack and his partner began to pray even more intensely than before that God would heal the woman. Each evening the girls attended the meetings. When asked how their mother was, they would report where in the seven- to nine-day cycle of the ailment their mother was. The morning visits continued. Then one evening the girls excitedly reported that the itching in their mother's hands and feet had stopped altogether.

The visits and prayers continued. The girls soon reported that their mother had no blisters and her hands and feet were beginning to heal. "What a great God we serve!" Jack declared.

The visits continued, and hope and joy began to replace the depression that had filled the home. "What a difference Jesus makes!" Jack and his partner exclaimed as they spoke of God's dealings with the woman.

One evening when the girls came to the meeting, it was obvious that something was wrong. Jack could not help noticing their sad faces. "What is the trouble this evening?" he asked as he shook their hands at the door.

"Mum has started itching again," came the despondent reply.

"We'll be back to see you girls and Mum tomorrow morning. Trust Jesus!" he confidently told them.

Actually, he had no idea what to say or do. What do you tell someone who has put their total trust in Jesus, who can't read the Bible, and yet has experienced the wondrous euphoria of divine healing, only to have the problem return? Jack called the entire evangelistic team together for special prayer. Most prayed through the entire night. Each one examined his or her own heart for anything that created a barrier between him or her and God.

"Am I taking any credit to myself for Your miracle of healing? Is there pride in my own heart? Are there hidden sins in my life that could be keeping the Holy Spirit from healing the woman?" Jack asked of God, and the others prayed similar prayers. They reminded God of how the woman had learned to trust Jesus all over again, and now the return of the disease had shattered her faith. They prayed for God to rebuke any satanic agency that might be working in her situation or in their own. After they had all prayed for removal of every obstacle they could think of, it was almost morning. Jack and his partner slept a couple hours before heading to her house about 9:00 a.m.

He felt himself in a quandary. What *would* he say? Should he tell her that healing was for people back in Bible times, but not for people today? Should he apologize for Jesus? Or for himself and the church? He was painfully aware of imperfections in his own life. Was this the reason the devil had regained a foothold in the woman's life? Engrossed in such thoughts, he didn't realize they were already at the house. Praying for guidance, he knocked on the door with a heavy, uncertain heart.

Suddenly the door flew open, and there stood Mum with the biggest smile he had ever seen on such a little woman. Jack knew something extremely special had happened. She thrust her hands out for him to see.

"Wha—?" He could hardly believe it, but it was true. Her hands were completely whole. They looked as fresh as a baby's, except for some flaking around the edges. While Jack stood speechless, Mum pushed him aside and ran out to the heavy cast-iron cooking pots, grabbed the handles, and lifted them high into the air. Obviously, not only had her hands been healed, but her feet as well. But Jack wanted to see to be sure.

"Praise God, Mum!" he said. "Praise God! This is His miracle! Would you show me the soles of your feet?"

She took off her sandals, and her feet had also healed. A thrill of holy awe swept over Jack. Body cells do not replenish themselves that fast, not in one night. Without doubt it was a miracle from God.

That night at the meeting he reported it to the people, and the good news electrified everyone. Word quickly spread throughout the area. The next Sabbath Mum walked the two miles to church on her own newly healed feet. Jack's evangelism students wrote a little song about it, which—though not terribly melodious—they sang for the remainder of the meetings and then back at the college for months to come. The whole student body seemed sobered and touched by such a revelation of God's power.

"My God can do anything!
Anything?
Anything!
My God can do anything!
He healed the sick;
He raised the dead;
He caused blind eyes to see!
My God can do anything!"

CHAPTER TWENTY-ONE

Rush and Run

I'm going riding," Steve shouted as he started out the door.

"You're not planning to ride Big Shane, are you?" his mother called back from the kitchen. Steve, with his penchant for animals, had taken riding lessons and proved to be an able young horseman, but Big Shane did have quite a reputation for being a difficult horse to handle.

"Mom, he really needs to be ridden. The Moores think that if we ride him enough, it will help him calm down. He does pretty well for me." A hint of braggadocio lurked in Steve's answer as he inched outside, hoping she would not try to squelch his afternoon plans.

"Well, do be careful," she acquiesced, knowing that boys, for some reason, must prove themselves. It was probably useless to say more anyway.

Catching the animal with a couple of sugar cubes was fairly easy, since a leather halter already hung around his huge head. Big Shane sidestepped and whinnied when Steve slung the saddle on top of the blanket on his back. The boy remembered to slap the horse's belly firmly with the strap as he tightened the cinch so the stubborn stallion's lungs would deflate. Now the saddle was secure. Steve knew all the horse's tricks. After Steve mounted Shane they headed up the road.

It was a beautiful Rhodesian day, perfect for riding. They broke into a gentle gallop. "Good going, Shane." Steve patted the horse's neck. But the animal was not feeling extremely cooperative, and he soon broke into a dead run. Steve decided to pretend running with the wind was exactly what he wanted to do—until he realized they were headed straight toward a wire fence. "Turn, Shane, turn," he coaxed, frantically pulling one rein. But instead of turning, the horse abruptly stopped—almost in mid-gallop—and the boy flew wildly over his head, striking his own head and landing on his back, breathless and stunned, on the hard dirt roadway.

Big Shane, relieved of his annoying load, now stood nonchalantly grazing nearby. Steve lay on the ground a few minutes, deciding if he could move or not. No one came to help him, so he tried to get up. "Wow, am I ever sore!" he moaned as he pulled himself to his feet and led the horse back to pasture.

The boy's back ached for months, but his parents were grateful that he had not been paralyzed or killed. Amazingly, the fall did not break any bones. "But don't anybody hug me!" he pleaded for several weeks.

Sabbaths were always special, and the younger Blancos helped to conduct branch Sabbath schools by riding on friends' motor scooters out to the bush country. Marion was actively involved in church activities also, conducting children's Sabbath school, entertaining visitors, visiting the sick, and accompanying Jack when he visited small church companies.

But everything was not idyllic in Africa. In addition to the normal challenges of mission service, cultural adaptation, and separation from loved ones, the family faced times of intense stress and grief at home, at school, and at work. Word came of the death of Jack's grandfather in Germany, followed by the death of his grandmother. During their second year of service, Jack and Marion received notification from the Rhodesian minister of education that "All alien children above Standard 3 (fifth grade) *must* be enrolled in an official school, or the entire family will be deported."

Send Cheri, only 12 years old, away to boarding school?

"You have the option of sending your daughter to the government boarding school in Bulawayo or your own boarding school in Gwelo" (several hundred miles away), the letter continued. Gas rationing and lack of a telephone would mean their only contact would be by mail until she came home for a break every three months. It was one of the hardest things they had ever done, but they felt they had no choice. They did their best to prepare her for life away from home and, thankful that she was mature for her age, entrusted her to God's care.

Letters spoke of her unhappiness, but they had expected an adjustment period. Then she came home on break, visibly shaken and sobbing bitterly. "I don't want to ever go back to that school! *Please* don't send me back!" Had they fully comprehended the insults, taunting, and even physical blows their daughter encountered from some of the boys because she was an American, their course would doubtless have been different. As it was, they tried to make life as normal and enjoyable as possible while she was at home, hardly mentioning school except to pray for her friends and tormentors.

On the day of her departure, her young shoulders heaved again with weeping and pleading. Jack, who had experienced so much pain and rejection in his youth, was in agony. The hearts of both parents nearly broke because they felt compelled to obey the government order.

They tried to cheer her and advise her on the best way to handle the discrimination she received. When the driver picked her up, there was a wrenching parting. She had stopped crying, but Jack could still see a lot of pain in her eyes. Cheri was having to go as an impressionable earliteen to a place where she was the brunt of unjustified animosity. A heavy burden for their children brought Marion and Jack before the Lord many times a day.

"Father," they prayed, "we're beginning to understand a little of how You must feel when Your children find themselves in difficult places. Please surround our daughter with Your love and peace. Make her a stronger person as a result of this experience. Help her to trust You."

Trips to Bulawayo dwindled to once a month because of the gas rationing. Necessities became scarce as England imposed economic sanctions and encouraged her allies to do the same. Reports circulated of riots and demonstrations, and the American government expressed concern for its citizens in Rhodesia. It placed the family on alert for possible evacuation if violence were to erupt. Grocery shopping became unnerving as the shelves became more and more empty.

"Just look at that, Steve!" Mom said on one of their monthly excursions to the Bulawayo grocery store. "They still don't have any oatmeal." The boy noticed that his mother had only a fraction of the groceries they usually bought. When they started to check out at the register, the cashier caught Marion's eye.

"I knew you always bought oatmeal, Mrs. Blanco," she said quietly, "so I saved you a box from a small shipment we got last week." She pulled a large, familiar-shaped box of Quaker Oats from behind the cash register. Probably not many 8- or 9-year-olds thank God for a box of oatmeal at the end of a day, but that evening Steve did. He began to understand that, most of the time, God uses *people* to answer prayers.

The next year another American girl joined Cheri at the mission school, and in their final year in Africa Cheri was able to remain at home, where she and her new friend took American correspondence courses. At that point the government didn't object, since the family was close to their scheduled departure time.

Jack continued to study himself during their African term. Not only was he chairman of the Theology Department of the college (often holding field schools of evangelism that the students were required to take), he was also pastor of the college church for a time. The mission school now encouraged him, as department chair, to work on his doctorate in theology. Any one of these responsibilities would normally be considered a full-time job. Perhaps because of his father's more-than-full schedule, Steve felt special when Jack took time in the evening to read extra Bible stories to him after dinner. Additionally, his dad read to him from the *How and Why* science books, greatly stimulating the youngster's interest in science. He knew his dad was an important man and totally committed to spreading the gospel, which they all understood took precedence over family matters. So many were vying for Dad's time and attention—yet he chose to be with his son when he could—a memory Steve still treasures.

But Jack was only human, and under the stress of his many roles, one Friday morning he became impatient with a couple of members of a college administrative committee. He considered them to be most unreasonable in their demands of what the church should do for the college. Becoming defensive, in his words, he "did not act very Christlike."

The printed bulletins already stated that he was preaching the next day on patience and Christian kindness. That fact made him feel terrible. How could he speak about patience and kindness when he had acted with neither? Friday afternoon and evening he prayed almost constantly. Sabbath morning he was still in agony, his family unaware of his struggle. The church service began, but Jack's mind was still on the incident from the committee, and he longed for a hole to open in the platform through which he could disappear.

Just before the sermon, a voice seemed to ask, "Why are you so upset? Are you here to preach your righteousness or Mine? Has your walk with Me gone to your head? Is your spiritual ego bothering you? I have called you to preach about Me, not you!"

Quietly he confessed to God his sin of spiritual pride and prayed for help to preach Jesus and His righteousness. When he stood behind the pulpit, he admitted, "I am far from perfect. Just yesterday I did not reflect Christ in a meeting. But praise His name, it is *His* patience and kindness, *His* understanding and forgiveness, *His* life and ministry that is to be our example now and forever. I stand rebuked."

Because of the Princeton degree, Jack gained ready acceptance at the University of South Africa in Pretoria. He spent parts of every summer and most other vacations in seminars at Pretoria. To complete his research dissertation, he awoke at 3:00 a.m. every day to get in four hours of study and writing before classes began. He stoically refused to think about the astronomical responsibilities he had taken on, repeating often, "My grace is sufficient for thee" (2 Cor. 12:9). After five years of intensive work he was able to graduate in absentia shortly after leaving the country. (The children will never forget spending so many vacations tenting in a Pretorian campground with no air conditioning after driving almost 500 grueling miles to get there.)

Once, while on a real vacation in a game park in Rhodesia, they learned that a lion had killed a giraffe nearby. They drove to the site and watched as the male lion ate his fill, snarling and growling impressively to keep the two females at a distance. The lionesses wandered right past the car while its inhabitants sat still and held their breath. The warden had told them to keep the windows closed, and the smell of gasoline would keep the animals from harming them.

When the male lion had had his fill, he lay down, and the females and cubs took over the carcass. Vultures watched from the treetops, circling now and again, impatient for their turn.

Marion and Jack planned to go home on furlough and then return to Africa. Robert H. Pierson, the division president, later (in 1970) to become the General Conference president, kindly and wisely advised them, "For the sake of your children's schooling, you really should go back to the United States and stay until they're older."

"Elder Pierson is right," Jack agreed. "I feel exhausted. A few months reacclimating ourselves to the U.S. before a new assignment is just what we all need."

"I can hardly wait," Marion agreed. "It will be good to just relax and enjoy friends and family. I am very tired."

But almost immediately an extremely urgent request came from the Philippines for Jack to head up the Philippine Union College's graduate program in religion. A sudden change in personnel had produced a vacancy that must be filled immediately. Jack and Marion prayed about it. Although they would have preferred not to go, seeing the great and urgent need, they ultimately accepted the call—a decision they afterward felt might have been a mistake in understanding God's direction.

Cheri, fortunately, was thrilled with the prospects of attending Far Eastern Academy. She'd heard glowing reports about it, and "Aunt" Jeané and "Uncle" Bob Jacobs would be like second parents to her. Jack and Marion tried to think of their new assignment as a change of pace. But they had worked extremely hard for five years and genuinely needed a time of rest to replenish their energy reserves. The constant pressures—or something—seemed to be gnawing at Jack. Severe stomach pain was becoming a near-constant companion.

His doctoral defense was not easy. One professor in particular was determined that no one holding to the seventh-day Sabbath would ever graduate from their program.

Another professor was kind, but questioned how Adventists could be so gullible as to believe in a present-day prophet who was obviously culturally influenced by her time. Jack quietly but firmly stood his ground. Had not biblical prophets been so influenced?

Through it all, his major professor stood by him. "But we had hoped to make a Dutch Reformed minister out of you," he later confided to Jack.

Perhaps making a real family vacation of their return to the U.S. would boost their spirits. Jack determined to make it a trip of a lifetime, for they might never have such an opportunity again. If they spent nights in cheap hotels and didn't eat much except bread and cheese, the rest of their general travel expenses from Africa to the U.S. would be covered. Why not make the most of it?

But first they must give away most of their goods, sell a few things to fellow missionaries, and pack the rest, which they then crated and shipped to Beira, a shipping port in Mozambique on the east coast of Africa. From there their things would travel to Philippine Union College.

So they said goodbye to their Solusi friends. On the way out of Africa, the family stopped in Salisbury so Cheri could take her final exams. The family then flew north toward Kenya on the first leg of their vacation. They enjoyed for a few days the sights of Nairobi, then boarded an Israeli airline, flying over parts of Ethiopia and Egypt as they headed toward Israel. The captain ordered the flight attendants to lower all window shades and turn off all lights. "We are flying over enemy territory," he explained.

The Six-day War between Israel and her Egyptian neighbors had only recently ended. Finally, when they were out of threatened air space, the lights came back on and the passengers could raise the shades. Shortly thereafter, the plane landed in Israel.

Visiting places where Jesus had actually walked was both exciting and disappointing. The children enjoyed riding camels, but most sites of biblical interest were so highly commercialized that they could hardly imagine Jesus being there—except for Nazareth and the Lake of Galilee. Sinai was off limits because of the recent war.

From Israel, they flew to Athens and visited where the apostle Paul had preached. Jack and Steve enjoyed a dinner together at an authentic Greek restaurant—that is, until intestinal upset struck with full force.

When those effects subsided, they all headed for Rome and saw where Paul had been imprisoned. They also visited the Vatican, but missed the Sistine Chapel and the pope's balcony appearance because of getting lost. From there they flew to central Europe to pick up the Volkswagen Jack had ordered. They spent some time touring Germany in the new station wagon.

"I'd like you to see the farm where I grew up, even though Grandmother and Grandfather died a few years ago," he told his family. He also showed them where he had been in labor camps, discovering to his dismay that the memories were still all too vivid. In Salzburg they saw where *The Sound of Music* was filmed, then sped west across Europe.

"The pizza in Italy tastes terrible!" Cheri declared, quite an expert now on restaurant food. The children had seen the book Mom had purchased entitled *Europe on $10 a Day.* They felt sure they came well under that daily budget. But there was so much to do free that they didn't waste time grieving over a lack of funds. It was an exciting and memorable time for the entire family.

The bread in Paris was wonderful, they all agreed. In Denmark the sun didn't go down until 11:00 p.m. and was up by 3:00 a.m., leaving them feeling strangely unrested. It became a family joke that the children had to taste ice cream in every country.

In Switzerland they climbed the lower Alps, enjoying the beautiful flowers and magnificent vistas. They hiked until they reached the snow, and the children, naturally, had to throw a few snowballs. When they reached the valley again, they were all so tired they almost collapsed from this strenuous workout called a vacation.

Next they headed for Berlin, but discovered it to be quite an experience driving through East Germany. Jack had to remove the license plates and buy special ones, then switch them back when they got out—all for a few hours' drive into East Germany and East Berlin. They saw the Wall, Check Point Charlie, and the Escape Museum. Communist guards were much in evidence, and the contrast between East and West was profound.

In East Berlin everything was drab and stark. Some buildings still had bullet marks from World War II in their walls. The

Blancos solemnly walked down Unter Dem Linden Street. A couple of blocks of department stores had a few things in their windows, but it was more like a ghost town. The family was glad to get past the border guards and their barbed-wire fences. The guards thoroughly searched every vehicle, rolling mirrors out on wheels to see under the automobile. They poked long stiff wires into gas tanks to ensure that no escapees were using them as a hiding place (with the real gas tanks being smaller and somewhere else in the car). It was a great relief to cross back into West Berlin (exchanging license plates again) and head to West Germany.

Leaving Berlin for West Germany, they accidentally made a wrong turn. After a while Jack noticed less and less traffic. Marion began to feel uneasy. "Aren't those Russian troops on that truck?" she asked.

Now they really became nervous, especially since they were driving a car with West German tags. Suddenly, they came to a lone soldier standing in the middle of the highway, checking traffic and signaling for them to stop. He spoke a few words of broken English and asked, "Where you are going?"

"To West Germany," Jack replied.

"You go wrong way. *Poland* that way." The soldier pointed in the direction they had been headed.

He allowed them to turn around, and they headed with great haste toward West Germany. They had wanted to see the Wartburg, where Martin Luther had translated the New Testament into German, but now there wasn't time to apply for permission to enter that part of East Germany. They dropped off their car to be shipped to the U.S. and flew to London, where they visited Newbold College, Buckingham Palace, and other historic spots. Now at last they were heading home.

Their plane landed at La Guardia Airport, and 12-year-old Steve, who had spent almost half his life in the bush of Africa, was in near shock. The wealth everyone seemed to have compared to the mud huts and grass roofs with which he was familiar awed him. He had been living with people who had only one or two changes of clothes and whose only transportation consisted of their feet. But in America even the poor seemed rich by comparison. He could not remember ever seeing so many cars.

Friends arrived to pick up the family at the airport. It was a hot August day, and Steve opened the back window of the car, hoping to catch a cool breeze once the car started moving. The driver commented on how hot it was and asked him to close the window so they could cool off. Did he misunderstand? Why would you close the window to cool off? That didn't make sense. So he left it open a few more minutes. She again asked him to close it, saying she would turn on the air conditioner. Reluctantly, he closed it, thinking, *I'm going to have to sit back here and swelter in this heat.* Suddenly a cold arctic blast burst from the dashboard. What would they think of next?

But the family hardly had time to appreciate being back in the States. The whirlwind vacation seemed only to increase in velocity. They picked up their VW at the dock and headed west to visit church members whom they had previously pastored, then on to be with family in Maryland, Michigan, and Chicago.

It amazed the children when they walked up to a grocery store and the front door opened automatically. And the food—row after row, aisle after aisle of beautifully arranged shelves stocked full of food, anything you could possibly want or imagine. All you had to do was pick it up, take it to the register, pay for it, and it was yours. No bare shelves, no ration stamps, no need to hide oatmeal behind the cash register for special customers.

In Africa they had not heard much world news, except when they got wind of something truly spectacular such as men landing on the moon, and that information came over shortwave radio. Here in America they noted that other families spent hours watching TV together, playing miniature golf, or going to the lake for a full-fledged, all-day picnic.

Almost as soon as they reached Chicago for a brief visit with Katie and Lee Blanco, it was time for Cheri to head for Far Eastern Academy. The school operated according to United States standards and consisted mainly of missionary children. The girl looked forward to the school year, but she was terrified of flying halfway around the world all alone at 15 years of age. As the plane sat on the runway of O'Hare Airport, her anxiety increased with each passing minute. She could tell from her watch that she was already going to miss the connecting flight from Los Angeles to Hawaii. What about her luggage—where would it be? Who would help her? How would she get to Japan and finally to Singapore if she didn't even make it to Los Angeles on time? She didn't know what to do and felt very much alone and extremely scared.

The emotional drain on her parents was hardly less. They had sensed her apprehension, but after committing her through prayer to God's care, they felt peace—unaware that she did not fully share in that comfort. She was, however, greatly relieved to discover in Los Angeles how well the airlines look after young passengers in her plight.

Jack and Marion met with the General Conference people and expressed concern about rushing over to the Philippines. Besides the upset of sending their young daughter away, they felt sluggish and exhausted. Jack's stomach pain still flared up. The General Conference scheduled physical examinations with an American physician. However, Jack, Marion, and Steve all passed their physicals without any difficulty and even received compliments on maintaining their good health while out of the country.

So with a lot of encouragement to move on and no obvious reason to stay, they headed west to California, stopping along the way to see some sights. Their last stop before their flight to the Philippines was San Francisco. Only later would they understand that their bodies were far more accurate in assessing their true condition than the physical tests had been.

Chapter Twenty-Two

The Philippines

Sir," the freight company representative told Jack in San Francisco when Blanco went to check on shipping their car, "the Philippines has just increased the tariff on cars imported to their country. You will have to pay an entry fee equal to what you originally paid for your car."

"But . . . but I just bought it *new* in Germany. That would be thousands of dollars, not even counting the cost of shipping it!" Jack was aghast. The General Conference, of course, could not concern itself with a missionary's decision to take or not take a car with him. It was up to him to figure out how to do it.

They had bought the car in Germany quite reasonably and, like other missionaries, thought they could take it overseas, use it in their next assignment, get a good price for it when they left, and hopefully be money ahead. In their case, it was not going to work that way. They faced either of two choices: pay an impossibly high import tariff to the Philippines or sell the car at a loss in the United States. They opted for the latter.

Jack, Marion, and Steve flew from San Francisco to Tokyo and spent a few days sightseeing and trying to relax. Ever since leaving Africa, Marion had felt cold and had to bundle up even though the weather had been warm everywhere they had been. Much later, they learned they should have recognized that as a symptom of a deeper problem. But now on to Hong Kong, where they shopped for clothes and other necessities.

Then they headed to Manila. Welcomed with open arms, they went to the campus of Philippine Union College, where they settled into a comfortable missionary house. Marion went to enroll Steve in seventh grade. "But he doesn't have a report card," the American teacher said.

"I was his teacher, and I can fill one out," his mother replied.

"But I understood he'd be in *sixth* grade, and I already have lesson plans prepared for sixth grade," the teacher insisted firmly.

"He did extremely well on a sixth-grade achievement test before we left, but he could take another test for you," Marion offered.

"No, I don't want to bother with that. Let's try him out in sixth grade and see how well he does." The teacher's voice had a ring of finality. Even though Jack also talked to her, the woman had made up her mind.

"Get such high marks that she'll change her mind," they encouraged their son. But nothing changed—except Steve's attitude toward school. His grades plummeted.

One of the first things Jack did at the college was to check over the graduate curriculum. Pastors and others from all over the Far Eastern Division and elsewhere had to complete their master's degree in four quarters. That's all their budgets allowed. So Jack had to begin teaching immediately, even though his curriculum materials and books had not yet arrived from Africa. He did the best he could to prepare for classes from the limited resources available in the library.

After they had been on the island only a few weeks, Typhoon Yoling, one of the worst in 20 years, hit the area. Steve was in school when it struck, shaking the little schoolhouse to its foundation. The wind ripped branches from trees and flung them through the air. Uprooted trees crashed to the ground. The teacher decided she must get the children to their nearby homes. Of course, they couldn't go alone, so some of the young, strong missionary men came to the rescue. Steve's escort grabbed his hand, and they went running out into the storm where debris flew all around. It was hard to see with dirt, grass, and leaves blowing in their faces. As they raced down the street in front of the publishing house, a large tree fell right across their path, barely missing them. When they jumped to get out of its way, the wind picked up Steve's slight, 80-pound body and tossed it into the air. His escort continued to run as he wrestled the youngster back to the ground.

People had warned the Blancos that the campus often got the fringes of typhoons, but this one hit full force, ripping the roof off the publishing house, taking part of the roof from the gym, and uprooting trees all over the campus. After the crashing and howling appeared to be over, Jack's family went outside to take pictures. A bit of sunshine broke through the calm clouds. Too calm. Suddenly Jack realized that they were momentarily in the eye of the storm, and he told everyone to run for cover. Then the reverse winds of the typhoon hit with almost demonic fury. The family barely made it back inside.

The devastation to the community after the storm was heartbreaking. The population around the compound had had simple little homes constructed of corrugated metal and held up by tree branches or small posts. The typhoon had flattened the structures, and many people lost their entire possessions. Of course, they didn't have insurance or money in the bank. One could never become accustomed to such grinding poverty.

Marion taught a class on the writings of Ellen G. White and also one in conversational English. She began taking classes again toward her master's degree in education. Also, she and Jack made a decided effort while in the Philippines to spend more time relaxing as a family. They took Steve out to Bataan and Corregidor where General McArthur's headquarters had been. Steve had fun exploring the nearby jungles with friends, going on trips in outrigger canoes to nearby islands, riding water buffalo, and playing in the rice paddies.

They also took time for picnics, a big thing with the Filipino people, who are extremely family-oriented. At one such picnic

Jack was not careful what he ate of the native cuisine and came down with a severe case of diarrhea. It left him feeling and looking drained. But he survived, and no one else in the family got it. Young Cheri came home for Christmas, and it was immensely satisfying to have the family together again. Happily, she seemed to be adjusting well to life at Far Eastern Academy.

Unfortunately, their household goods had still not arrived. Finally, Jack went to the union mission treasurer. "We have a problem," he began.

"Oh?"

"Yes. We've been in the Philippines for four months now, and none of our goods have arrived from Africa. What do you suggest we do?"

The treasurer immediately contacted Africa and found that the Blanco possessions were still sitting on the open dock in Mozambique. It would be another two weeks before they would arrive in the Philippines—five months since being shipped from Solusi.

To add to their problems, Jack now received a letter from the U.S. government that stated: "This is to notify you that you must pay U.S. import duty on the VW that you sold in the United States, since you did not merely drive it through going to the Philippines. This import tax is due immediately, including interest."

Eventually, Jack did buy a used car, "held together with safety pins," the family joked. Driving in Manila is different from most anywhere else in the world, and he learned quickly that he must drive offensively (using that term both in the football as well as the politeness sense) in order to get anywhere. Most of the time he would be only inches away from another car, but whoever's car nose was an inch ahead won, and the other driver would acquiesce. Drivers moved back and forth into whatever lane gave them the best advantage. Despite that, Jack got only one little nick on his front fender the entire time they were there. Of course, no one bothered to call the police to report an accident—the authorities couldn't possibly get through the traffic.

Finally Jack and Marion received word that their goods had arrived in Manilla. Patiently they waited several days for someone to deliver them to their house, but the shipping containers continued to sit on the Manilla dock. It seemed the company had no intention of transporting them out to the campus, even though Jack had already paid for that service. He called the officials, but still nothing happened. Then he phoned the union treasurer again.

"Well, Jack, I'm reasonably sure the local customs people are waiting for a tip—you know, a little 'pocket money,' a payment under the table," the treasurer said.

"But that's illegal!" Jack protested. "I can't do that. Just imagine if I got caught! I can see the headlines. It would be an embarrassment to the college and to the church. I simply can't *do* that!"

The treasurer was much calmer, perhaps because it wasn't his possessions sitting on the dock. "Jack, it *is* against the law, you're right. But the government knows it happens, and they wink at it. Customs people are generally underpaid, so they're allowed to 'collect' tips as they can on the side, and nothing is done about it. If you really want your things, I suspect that's the only way you're going to get them."

So with his heart in his throat, Jack took some money, went down to the dock on Friday afternoon, requested that their possessions be released and delivered Monday, and then "tipped" the official. The very next day—Sabbath morning—their household goods arrived at their house. It must have seemed a bit odd to everyone walking to church (held in the gymnasium across the street from the Blanco home) to see huge crates being unloaded at the home of the head of the Religion Department on Sabbath morning.

Sunday morning they eagerly began tearing open the crates. A Filipino man helping them pulled a board partially free, then braced his foot against the contents and pushed and pulled. His foot went crashing through a favorite wall picture. When they had all the crates opened and the rest of the contents pulled out, Marion discovered that termites had destroyed many of their things. However, determined to be cheerful, the family gave thanks for what had safely arrived—and for what they had given away before leaving. At long last, they could return the dishes, cookware, and linens that kind fellow missionaries had lent them.

Jack had come to the Philippines to help with the graduate school, and he was intent on doing that. From the beginning he noticed that the courses making up their graduate degree program were rather general in nature rather than focused on Adventist theology and biblical studies. No doubt previous administrators had done it that way because the government had to approve everything for the degree program. So he asked the government officials if the school could change some of the college courses. "Submit class outlines, and we'll see," came the reply.

So he produced about a dozen class outlines and short syllabi and submitted them to the government and waited. A few months later the government rejected his modifications.

His next move was to try to get the program accredited by ATSEA, the Association of Theological Schools of South East Asia. It would upgrade the graduate school of religion to a seminary. If he could accomplish that, the school could offer its own Bible courses without interference from the government. Although it took a lot of time and a lot of work, he finally completed the required paperwork, and under the next administration the school became accredited by ATSEA.

The current administration also had started investigating possibilities of moving the campus and making the college into a university. Along with the chairman of the board, Jack must have looked at 60 different properties, one being through a jungle, then almost straight up to the flat top of a mountain. Eventually they discovered a suitable piece of property that the church later developed into a new campus.

The Philippines has three seasons: hot, hotter, and hottest. To escape the heat, missionaries used small cabins the division owned about a hundred miles away up in the mountains at Baguio. The Blancos spent a weekend there at Christmas and again in early summer. The cooler air invigorated the rest of the family, but Marion nearly froze. Even with four army blankets piled on her, she was still cold.

Then that summer illness and despair struck with a vengeance. After their trip to the mountains, Marion developed laryngitis that just would not go away. She had it while Cheri was home for the summer, so the 16-year-old taught her mother's class in conversational English to the Filipinos until the time came for her to return to Singapore.

One morning after Cheri had left, Jack was having his private devotions. The pressure and stress they had been under so long seemed to well up and overwhelm him. Thoughts flooded his mind that he could not brush aside.

What his family had gone through now seemed simply too much. For five years in Africa they had driven themselves, only to discover they couldn't even use their earned furlough. The climate change from dry Africa to the damp Philippines demanded adjustment; the graduate program for pastors desperately needed more focus on the distinctiveness of what Seventh-day Adventists believe, and would require extensive negotiations with the government plus mountains of paperwork; classes were about to begin again; the college president had gone on furlough back to the States and left him in charge; his daughter was 1,500 miles away in Singapore; his son was having difficulty at school; Marion needed medical attention; the business about the car still caused problems—and on it went. *Have I not gone the second and even the third mile for the church? Who appreciates it or even says thank you? Why on earth am I doing all this?*

He felt devastated. *If that's how the General Conference*

treats its missionaries, then forget it. And if this is how the church treats its people, they can have it. I'm going home. And the ministry? Well, if that's what the ministry is all about, they can have that, too. I'm quitting!

The next thought was so horrifying that it shook him to the bone. *If that's the way Christ treats me, forget it!* The thoughts and emotions had tumbled after each other so quickly, he felt out of control. As he knelt, trying to pray, he felt stunned. "Is this *me* thinking this way?" he asked himself. "Forsaking Christ?"

Never in his converted life would he have imagined that such thoughts would enter his head. He started to weep. For a long time he cried to the Lord for forgiveness, confessing his weakness. Had he become like Peter—proud of his commitment, his service to the Lord? "Though they all leave Thee, I will not?" He felt that for a brief moment he had denied his Lord. The pain inside was agonizing. But it was almost time to go to class. Washing his face and saying nothing to anyone, he forced breakfast down to avoid questions.

Although he smiled to his expectant students, inside he was still agonizing. "Am I a hypocrite?" No, he had remained true to his Lord and had not given in to his emotions. Pointing his students to Jesus restored Jack's own faith and confidence in Him. Days passed, and the pain gradually eased. He realized that he was looking again to Jesus for confidence and not to himself. Never again would he trust himself to be loyal to Christ in and of himself. He had absolutely nothing to offer his Saviour—not even a guarantee that he would never leave Him. Jack simply did not have the faith, the ability to cling to God. All he could do was to believe in his Father's ability to hold on to him and never let him go.

After Cheri had returned to school in Singapore, the campus doctor discovered a lump in Marion's neck and sent her to Manila Sanitarium for treatment as an outpatient. The nurse, trying to be helpful, applied heat to the lump, then thoroughly and vigorously massaged it. But nothing helped. When Marion went to see a specialist, he said, "You also have a lump on your vocal cords, and it should be removed first." She checked in at the hospital, and the specialist received special permission to operate there.

They screwed her mouth open with a metal device, but did not put it in right and it chipped the edge off her front tooth. She tried to tell them what was wrong, but the laryngitis kept her from speaking and she couldn't use her arms because they had been strapped down. The surgery proved there was no cancer on the vocal cords. However, it did not correct the problem of the other lump. After the specialist spent an hour and a half displaying his shoddy work, the hospital barred him from doing further surgery there.

"The only thing left to do is to operate on the lump itself to see if it's cancerous or not," another surgeon declared. Surgery was again scheduled. The doctor told Jack, "If the surgery doesn't take long, you'll know it's not cancer, but if it continues a long time, it will be because it is cancer."

A college board meeting had been scheduled on the same day as Marion's surgery at the union office right next to the Manila Sanitarium. Because the college president was still on medical leave in the United States, the responsibility fell to Jack to be at the board meeting. He and Marion discussed it, and both felt confident that since the operation on the vocal cords had shown no cancer, the neck surgery would in all probability prove likewise. "Yes, Jack," she said, "you definitely should attend the board meeting. I'll be asleep anyway. Then I'll be waiting for you in my hospital room when it's over."

At noon when the board meeting dismissed, Jack hastened to the hospital, expecting to greet his smiling wife. Before reaching her room, he met the American general physician. "How's Marion?" he asked expectantly.

"She's still in surgery—since 7:00 this morning. It doesn't look good, Jack," the doctor said. "She probably won't be out for another hour, at least." That gave Jack time to drive back home and pick up Steve. The two of them hurried back to the recovery room. It was cancer, and the surgeon had removed a large portion of her neck. Marion was all bandaged up and heavily sedated, with tubes seeming to come and go everywhere. Of the eight lymph nodes removed, two had metastasized with two different kinds of cancer.

The sight of his mother visibly shook Steve. Jack, stunned, fought back the tears and prayed silently. What did it all mean? Would his wife, who had stood by his side through many lonely hours, now be snatched from life? She had so much to live for. Their son, Steve, just now maneuvering into the turbulent teen years, needed his mother. Cheri, an ocean away at Far Eastern Academy—how would she handle this?

Jack alternately stood and sat by his wife's bed for hours. Intravenous feeding was all that was allowed her the first day, but the next day the nurse brought in fluids so Marion could try swallowing. Of course, she was eager to prove she could do it. But her epiglottis refused to function at all, and the liquid went down her windpipe, sending her into a choking and coughing fit. What did it all mean?

By the third day Marion still couldn't even swallow her saliva without spasms of uncontrollable choking. The surgeon walked into the room and sat down. "I had to cut out quite a bit of the right portion of her neck," he explained rather matter-of-factly, "including part of the jugular vein on that side. The six-hour surgery went well." He indicated that it could easily have cost her her voice or had her talking like a man. To him, the epiglottis problem seemed minor.

"Is it possible she won't ever be able to swallow again?" Jack asked.

"It's possible," he admitted as he rose and hurriedly left the room.

Jack and Marion looked at each other in bewilderment. He took her frail hand in his, and kneeling beside her bed, began to pray. Marion joined her silent prayer with his. "Dear Lord, please help us. Help Marion's epiglottis to work. We know You can do all things. Help us to trust You more fully."

After prayer they squeezed each other's hands and then reluctantly opened their eyes. Marion swallowed tentatively, then reached for the cup with the straw, took a sip of water, and swallowed again. The water went down, and she didn't choke. As they praised God, they knew they would never count it mere coincidence. It was a special miracle just for them that they would never forget.

However, the problem did not end. The next day the American doctor came to see Marion, his face and voice serious. "The division has voted to send you to Loma Linda for treatment," he said abruptly.

It shocked her, since neither she nor Jack had even requested such a thing.

"Since the cancer is in the lymph system and has already metastasized," the physician continued, "you'll need much more extensive treatments than we can give you here. The best place to take those treatments is at Loma Linda University hospital. The arrangements may take a little time."

"Jack can't leave now," she protested. "He's got work to do at the college. I—I can go alone and come back when I'm well."

The doctor smiled, touched her partially paralyzed face, and said gently, "You know, you can't even raise your right arm now. No, your husband and son must go with you."

The hospital released her. Under her direction, Jack and Steve began to pack what others might later have to ship home for them. Everything was happening so fast that they felt as if they were in a mental fog, as if they would awaken from a bad dream.

After saying goodbye to the busload of friends who came to wish them well, Jack, Marion and Steve, adorned in leis, boarded the huge 747 packed with passengers, including many servicemen from Vietnam.

"Do you think this plane will be able to lift off the ground with all these people on board?" Marion wondered aloud.

Air Force veteran that he was, Jack smiled indulgently. "Yes, dear. Just relax. God will take care of us."

Chapter Twenty-Three

Ah, Home?

"Ladies and Gentlemen, I regret to announce that we have a problem with one of the engines and must return to Manila for repairs," the pilot's voice came over the intercom about an hour and a half into the flight.

A passenger behind them who was also a pilot leaned forward and pointed out the window. "See that engine over there? That's the one that isn't working!"

Jack and Marion reached for each other's hands, looked down at the vast Pacific Ocean, and prayed quietly. Gratefully, they arrived without mishap back in Manila. Some friends heard what had happened and returned to the airport to spend more hours of waiting with them. Finally, the Blancos reboarded, and the plane took off the second time. In Guam it made an unscheduled stop because the engine needed repairing again, so once more they sat in the airport terminal and waited. In Hawaii the same thing happened. Here they had the opportunity to change planes (which they eagerly did), and after more than 25 hours without sleep, they finally landed in Los Angeles. Marion was exhausted.

Within a few days they found a small house to rent, and Steve commenced seventh grade in yet another new school. The doctors started Marion's treatments immediately. The cancer had originated in her thyroid, explaining why she had felt cold even in a warm climate. They learned that the physical she had had after their return from Africa would have detected it if the physicians had administered a simple thyroid test. But now the cancer had spread throughout her system. After days of tests, the physicians decided that they must destroy any remnant of thyroid left in her body.

Before she was hospitalized, Jack and Marion requested anointing. Elder Lehmann, pastor of the Campus Hill church, and Elder E. L. Minchin, participated. All present in the hospital prayer chapel had full confidence that God had heard their prayers, but how He chose to answer, they would leave to His love and wisdom.

Marion was admitted to Loma Linda Hospital and given a special insulated, sanitized room. Plastic sheets labeled "radioactive" were taped all over the floor. No one was allowed in except the doctors. They entered her room looking like spacemen, wearing body suits, helmets, gloves, and masks. They carried a shielded bottle of "atomic cocktail" (radioactive iodine) with a straw in it. All Jack could do was watch from the observation window as his tiny wife, sitting meekly on the edge of her sterile white bed, drank the radioactive substance. They warned her that she might end up vomiting, so they kept the path to the bathroom clear.

Slowly she sipped the drink while Jack prayed and the doctors watched. Each long moment stretched into another. Marion, thankfully, did not become nauseated. After she finished, the doctors left and closed the door behind them. Marion waved to Jack at the window, then lay down and went to sleep. Since she was temporarily radioactive, the staff constantly monitored her for three days and then released her. By that time, she was extremely weak. Jack had to carry her from place to place around their house. After regaining some strength, she underwent tests for two more weeks. The tests revealed that, amazingly, no trace of thyroid cancer remained in her body.

Now she took thyroid medication in order to bring her body chemistry back to normal. It was possible that it could also cause the cancer to recur, so there was still some uneasiness. The physicians would conduct another test in six months.

Still unable to raise her right arm, Marion finally went to see a neurologist. After careful examination, he said, "I'm afraid the nerve has been severed. There is nothing we can do."

However, the physical therapist at the Loma Linda School of Health said, "We can often do things doctors can't do." He recommended swimming in a heated pool and daily exercise. But after a month, even he declared that there had been no progress and nothing more could be done.

That same night, January 11, 1972, Marion lay awake long after Jack fell asleep. It was the day the Far Eastern Division had written that they would be praying especially for her. "Dear God, please hear the prayers of all Your dear people. I really need a blessing from You just now. If only You would help me raise my right arm, I would know that my cancer is gone." No sooner had she expressed that desire to God than she got out of bed and promptly raised *both* arms over her head.

"Jack, wake up! *Look!* Look at what God has done!"

Now that Marion seemed on the mend, Jack felt it was time to look for what might be causing the pain around his stomach. The doctors in Africa had not found anything, neither had the American physician at his Stateside physical, nor the doctors in Manila. Although examined again in Loma Linda, tests there also proved negative or inconclusive. One physician thought Jack might have ulcers, but another argued that he didn't have the classic symptoms. Since Marion's future health was still in doubt and Jack himself wasn't well, the General Conference ultimately decided they should stay in the States rather than return to the Philippines. They received some of the furlough time they had not been able to take after coming back from Africa. For several months they simply rested and waited for her final tests while Marion got stronger. Jack took Steve places that would especially interest a young person, such as Disney World, Sea World, and Knott's Berry Farm.

The job question began to weigh heavily on Jack's mind. He had no idea where they would go from Loma Linda. "Remember how we trusted God to lead when you finished seminary?" Marion reminded him. He decided she was right—God was still in control.

Finally, an offer came to teach at Columbia Union College, near Washington, D.C. They had bought an old station wagon that they now drove east, after contacting friends in the Philippines and asking them to ship the remainder of the family's household goods to Baltimore. Steve spent a month with his grandparents, Katie and Lee, at the restaurant in Chicago while his parents got settled. Back in Maryland, Jack and Marion moved into a friend's house for a month until they could find an apartment of their own.

Soon Cheri returned from Far Eastern Academy to complete her final academy year in Takoma Park, and Steve completed the eighth grade. Both teens began working after school and contributing toward their tuition and clothing expenses.

Jack taught classes at both the college and the academy. It was quite a challenge and a culture shock after teaching highly motivated ministers in the Orient to attempt to teach freshman college students of the mid-1970s, not to mention senior academy students. The experience tested the entire family's flexibility after living in and adapting to other countries and cultures for almost seven years.

They looked for a house to buy and were astounded that the price of houses had nearly doubled from only the year before. A home of their own was totally out of the question. They had no credit rating and did not qualify for loans. Nor had they any credit cards. Secretly they wondered if they shouldn't have kept the house they had turned over to the conference seven years previously.

Finally they scraped together barely enough for a tiny down payment on their portion of an 18-unit townhouse where many General Conference employees, mostly returning missionaries, were building and buying. Someone trusted the entire group with a mortgage, and together with 17 others, they signed jointly for the bank loan. It would be a year before the building would be finished enough for them to move in, so the Blancos leased an apartment.

Meanwhile, Jack's stomach pain continued. One physician suggested an endoscopy (putting a tube down the throat) so they could see what was going on. It revealed ulcers hidden in the folds of the duodenum, at the exit from the stomach. They had ulcerated and healed repeatedly, leaving scar tissue that now constricted the duodenum and made it difficult for food to exit the stomach. The physicians scheduled surgery even though they were unsure whether they would remove the duodenum and part of the stomach or if they would simply cut out the ulcerated area from the duodenum and bring the opening back to normal. As it turned out, they followed the latter course, and after five days in the hospital, Jack returned home.

Marion had recovered, and she began working in the hospital as unit manager. Jack was again experiencing the joys of teaching full-time and seeing young people give their hearts to God. The troubled months of his recent life began to fade into memory, and he began to feel useful again.

The children were not fully over their adjustment periods, however. Cheri found it somewhat confining living at home after being on her own for several years. Steve began to immerse himself in an exciting and enticing world he had not known in developing countries. With his own overseas accent, ignorance of American culture, and naive curiosity, it was natural that he felt most acceptance from more free-spirited fellow teens who were also not the most conforming Christian youth in the seventies. He admits to a couple of years of wildly rebellious behavior while in Takoma Park, often embarrassing his parents. It seemed for a while that God had turned a deaf ear to his parents' daily prayers for their son. But in Steve's words, "Dad's patience in guiding, counseling, and encouraging was crucial in guiding me back."

The "Life and Teachings of Jesus" classes were usually large at the college, and a favorite for Jack to teach. It thrilled him to watch young lives change when immersed in studying the life of Christ. A young non-Adventist nursing student, Stephanie,* reluctantly joined the class. She had determined not to be influenced by the Adventist religion, and Jack could clearly read that fact from the adamant look on her face. However, as the class continued to study and discuss the life of Christ in the Gospels, she slowly relaxed her animosity. Days turned into weeks, and she obviously was becoming more interested. She began to show a certain eagerness by leaning forward in her seat. A few weeks before the end of the semester she approached her teacher after class and asked, "Doctor Blanco, could I please talk with you?" He invited her to come to his office.

"I have really been enjoying this class," she began.

"Well, I'm very glad to hear that," he smiled. "Stephanie, I believe you have come to know Jesus recently—am I right?"

"Oh, yes!" she replied enthusiastically. "I have just given my heart to Him."

"Praise the Lord!" Jack responded.

"I really want to thank you for what you have shown me—not only in the subject matter for the class, but for exemplifying the life of Christ in your own," she said. "I only wish I could be as good a Christian as you."

"Stephanie, you will grow to be more and more like Jesus," Jack answered, "but you must not focus too much on your shortcomings or on what you perceive to be the goodness of others." (In his heart Jack knew how far short he fell of God's ideal for him.) "Make Jesus the focus of your life. He is the only one deserving our praise. Giving your heart to Jesus is like allowing Him to plant a seed in your heart. The tree is already in the seed. It only needs watering and feeding, and it will grow into a tree—a mighty tree for Him. Remember, the tree is in the seed."

---

*Not her real name

Stephanie seemed to understand, and they knelt and prayed and both committed themselves anew to Jesus. She was only one of many who made his teaching so fulfilling.

After two years in the Religion Department, the school asked Jack to serve as academic dean, which he did for the next three years. Cheri graduated from college, married a premed student, and moved to Loma Linda. Steve graduated from academy and left for Southern College to take the premed course.

Most of the Columbia Union College administration thought that the institution should move to a new location because of increasing crime in the area. Nursing students had to have security guards accompany them the one block from the dorm to the hospital for fear of robbery or rape. As dean of the college, Jack supported a move, realizing that the school would probably never grow and prosper in its existing location.

The conference put a down payment on 800 acres next to a 3,000-acre state park, with the intention of transferring the school, but it was not to happen. A 500-member constituency meeting decided by a margin of about 20 votes to keep the college where it was as the one and only city college in the North American Division. The popular thing at that time was ministering to inner-city needs, and some felt that a city college helped meet that mission. The decision disappointed Jack and many others.

About the same time he accepted an offer to be associate editor of the *Adventist Review*. Though he didn't feel his talents lay in this direction, the management team insisted that what they needed was his solid theology background. While he was at the Review, his stepfather, Lee Blanco, passed away, and Katie came to live with them. Jack and Marion welcomed her warmly and made every effort to make her feel as comfortable as possible. When she joined them for their first family worship, Jack read the first chapter of Genesis from *The Living Bible*. "What happened to the seventh day?" was her immediate question.

"We'll read about that tomorrow," her son smilingly responded, rejoicing at her growing desire to learn from God's Word.

Marion worked at the General Conference as a secretary, so it was a busy household every morning as they scurried about.

One morning Katie did not come down for breakfast, and Marion suggested that Jack take a tray of food up to her before they left for work. He went up to his mother's bedroom, slowly opened the door, and saw her still sleeping. She looked so peaceful that he hated to wake her, but knew he had to. So he set the tray down and said, "Mother, we have to leave now, but Marion has fixed your breakfast. I'll leave it on the table right next to you in case you want to rest a bit longer."

No response.

"Mother? Mom?" She did not so much as flutter an eyelid. Jack took her hand to shake her, and then he realized she was dead. Totally unexpected and sudden, it must have happened not long before, because her body was still warm. They called the rescue squad, who tried to revive her, but it was too late. She had died of a massive heart attack. On her bedside was the Protestant Bible she had been reading. Looking back later, Jack and Marion understood the experience as a blessing because of the number of moves they had to make shortly thereafter. It would have been difficult for Katie Blanco to have adjusted to them. They realized they never had to look far to see, even in pain and loss, God's love abundant with mercy.

After a year and a half at the Review, Jack realized that sitting behind a desk all day reading papers was not for him, and he requested permission to pursue a position back into teaching or pastoring. Before long he received an invitation to pastor, first in Johnson City, Tennessee, then in Palm Springs, California. Returning to pastoring after 15 years in education revealed that the rewards of pastoral ministry had not changed. The emphasis was still on family—the joyous baptisms, births, weddings, and answers to prayers. And, of course, there came also the inevitable sorrows of sickness, suffering, and death.

However, some things had altered. Years before when he had associated with other ministers in local ministerial associations, he had heard a lot of quiet talk about the problems of divorce, drugs, alcohol, etc. It was rare that those problems surfaced in Adventist congregations. The big concerns in the late fifties and early sixties were where to hold the next evangelistic meeting and where to build the next church. Now in the late seventies and early eighties the same problems that had plagued other denominations had become widespread in Adventist churches too.

But in spite of changes, the rewards of ministering to God's people remained the same. Whether Jack knelt on the cow-dung floor of an African family, on a floor mat with a Filipino family, or on the plush carpet of a Palm Springs family, he found the needs of people—of families—were much the same. When he prayed for the father, the mother, the children—he could sense the Holy Spirit's presence in people's responses. Hearts and lives were transformed, and that was all that mattered.

Life in California was delightful. Cheri, less than two hours away, worked as a child nutritionist in San Bernardino County and then taught at the Loma Linda University School of Health while her husband finished medical school. Steve graduated from Southern and visited his parents in Palm Springs after Loma Linda's School of Medicine accepted him, but a change in government policy made it financially prohibitive for him to attend there. Reluctantly, he returned to Tennessee, where educational expenses were more affordable. Marion served as the church secretary.

Then Jack received feelers about going to Southern College, Pacific Union College, and Southwestern Union College. It was not an easy choice. Cheri and her husband were in California. Steve was still at Southern, exploring various options for medical school. Jack and Marion did not want to make a choice of where to serve God based on their own desires. Where did the Lord want them to be?

CHAPTER TWENTY-FOUR

Southern Skies Seem Always Blue

As they prayed, they felt God was leading them to accept the offer at Southern College. (Cheri and her husband eventually settled in Hinsdale, Illinois, where he joined a pathology group. Steve graduated from East Tennessee State University, took specialized training at the University of Virginia, and established his practice in Nashville, Tennessee.)

The college warmly welcomed the Blancos, but enrollment that had peaked a couple years before now turned downward, as happened with many other private colleges. Turbulent theological issues disturbed the constituency, and certain teachers and concepts came under scrutiny and attack, sometimes unjustified. Concern, not always Christlike, surfaced from many quarters. It created much additional work for Jack the first couple years, coupled with heavy teaching schedules during the school year as well as in the summer, not to mention involvement in camp meetings and other speaking appointments. But Jack was willing to do whatever was necessary to help rebuild confidence in the school.

Shortly after arriving at Southern, he developed prostate problems. As he lay in his hospital bed after surgery, the doctor walked into his room and said, "I think you might have cancer, but it will be a few days before we know for sure." Then he casually turned and left the room.

Jack lay there stunned. They had just come to Collegedale, and now this? The next few days were anxious ones filled with prayer. Again he and Marion praised the Lord when the results came back negative.

Later Marion suddenly developed severe pain in her abdomen. Even after numerous tests and antibiotics, the pain persisted month after month. The only solution seemed to be exploratory surgery, a difficult decision because of her previous experiences. This time Jack waited in her room for the report. When he answered the phone, the nurse on the other end said, "Everything went fine, Mr. Blanco, but the doctor would like to talk to you."

Jack feared a serious problem had developed, and he began imploring God anew. When the doctor appeared a few minutes later, he explained, "Jack, apparently Marion's appendix ruptured about seven months ago. It infected her gallbladder and then somehow sealed itself off. We found the large mass that we think was causing her pain and removed it. Now it looks like everything is going to be OK."

The accompanying nurse added, "She must have had Someone upstairs looking after her!"

Jack could hardly believe it—another wondrous blessing from his heavenly Father. And most of it occurred when they weren't even aware of a problem! It took several months for Marion to feel normal again.

Shortly after he began teaching on the beautiful Southern campus, Jack felt a personal need to renew his own devotional life. "I have no right to teach religion unless I know Jesus Christ personally and anew each day," he told his wife. While he had absorbed knowledge and training that helped him convey religious information without difficulty, he knew that much brighter minds than his had lost their way because they did not keep vibrant their own personal relationship with Jesus. He pondered and prayed over how best to do that. Feeling impressed to study a book of the Bible about Christ (Mark, to begin with, because it is the shortest of the four Gospels), he began to write out his understanding of what each verse was saying.

It was a slow process, but since it was only for his own personal growth, that did not matter. He focused on the central thought of each verse. *How would Jesus say it if He were here now? If I met Him in the office, at the mall, in the garden—or if He were riding with me in the car, how would He say the same thing He said years ago in a different culture and place?*

Using a computer would have been faster, but somehow that didn't seem appropriate. So he wrote out his verse-by-verse understanding of the entire book of Mark by hand, scratching out words and sentences until, to his own mind, it was clear what the passage meant. If a passage was extremely difficult, he would do further research, but for the most part, he kept it pure devotional time. He had no thought of ever publishing anything. Usually he rose about 4:00 a.m., sometimes 3:00 to work on it, and often became so involved with it that he forgot the time. Marion reminded him to get ready for breakfast and classes.

In those early-morning moments he felt himself there with Jesus beside the Lake of Galilee, in Judea, on Calvary. His paraphrasing brought him renewed power and energy each day. After the Gospel of Mark proved such a personal blessing, he did another New Testament book, and in a little more than three years he completed the entire New Testament.

One Christmas he showed the handwritten notes to his children, sharing with them what he'd been doing and the blessing he had received. Steve's wife said, "Why, Dad, I would love to have a copy of this for a Christmas present. This is *very* special and beautiful."

"Hmm, that would be a pretty large order," he answered. "You couldn't possibly follow all the scratching and marginal notes. I'll have to transcribe it. Let's see what I can do for *next* Christmas."

Once he began transcribing, however, typing again did not prove to be a devotional experience for him. To him, devotional time should connect your heart with Jesus. Typing out religious information on a computer didn't seem to qualify. So in his spare time he did transcribe the New Testament paraphrase he had written. But for his own private devotions, he started writing out the Old Testament verse by verse just as he had the New.

Others saw the transcript and encouraged him to have it published. Eventually, the College Press printed 5,000 copies of the New Testament.

In 1987 Southern asked Jack to become chairman of the Religion Department. Dr. Gordon Hyde, his predecessor, had established a firm spiritual foundation, and after praying about it, Jack enthusiastically determined to accept the new responsibility and do his best for his Lord. (The number of religion and theology majors has doubled since that time.)

In 1989 Jack and Marion's first grandchild, Derek, was born to Cheri and her husband. Steve and his wife presented them with Chelsea in 1991.

Now people started asking when he would publish the rest of the Bible. It took seven years to complete his verse-by-verse study of the Old Testament, and Jack knew even then it was not in publishable form. He was overwhelmed with the task of getting it to that stage when someone he hardly knew called and asked if she could help with editing—without pay, of course. Jack was so incredulous at her offer that he almost forgot to ask how much experience she had at such things.

When he found she had never done such a project, it didn't deter him. "If God can use me to write it, He can use you to edit it," he told Jolena King in his office. "Let's pray for His guidance." Marion had come to help him determine if the woman was a legitimate volunteer sent from the Lord. After prayer, he handed his new volunteer (who thought she would be one of many) a rough manuscript of the book of Job. Eventually a couple of willing typists appeared. It took almost two years to get the manuscript ready for publication, and in spite of some proofing errors that surfaced after publication, they had done their best as an offering to God.

The first edition of *The Clear Word* came off the press in 1993. Gratifying letters have poured in from readers who tell how the Holy Spirit has used it to reach their own hearts or the hearts of relatives who had been spiritually cold and indifferent, who had found the Bible so difficult to read that they had quit trying, or who had previously pictured God as stern and accusing rather than loving and kind.

Although some have questioned the paraphrase, this does not trouble Jack. "God has a thousand ways—none needing human approval—to lead people to understand His love," he says. "We just need to be sure we are open to His guidance—and, yes, people do need to be cautious what they accept. Hold everything to the standard, 'To the law and to the testimony: if they speak not according to this word, it is because there is no light in them' [Isa. 8:20]."

Jack pledged every cent of royalty from the sale of *The Clear Word* for ministerial scholarships. He remembers what it was like in his own life trying to balance crushing financial needs while attending school.

One day as Jack and his wife were leaving church, a woman tapped him on the shoulder and said, "Dr. Blanco, I want you to meet my friend, Jana, who is studying for baptism as a result of reading *The Clear Word.*" Such experiences happen frequently, and Jack's response is always the same: "Praise the Lord!"

Since coming to Southern in 1983 Dr. Blanco has served as professor, department chair, and now dean of the School of Religion, as well as president of the Adventist Theological Society (which he founded) and president of the Southeastern Chapter of the Evangelical Theological Society.

He and his colleagues established the R. H. Pierson Institute of Evangelism and World Mission. Through it the School of

Religion has developed the *"College of the Air* radio program beamed by Adventist World Radio to believers in China. The R. H. Pierson Institute also allows Southern teachers to spend time training pastors at the Zaoksky Seminary in Russia.

Southern College became Southern Adventist University in 1996. The Department of Religion became the School of Religion. Currently it has the largest body of religion majors in the North American Division. Placement rates for theology graduates at Southern have ranged between 95 and 100 percent. Faculty members pray often with and for their students. Two summer field schools have excellent student participation and generally result in 35 to 185 baptisms each summer.

"Quietly, gently, Jack Blanco has provided the steadying, conservative leadership necessary to consistently hold true to the biblical doctrines and theology with which Seventh-day Adventists are familiar," says former Southern Adventist University president Dr. Don Sahly. "As a gentleman and a scholar, he has exemplified every aspect of what a loving Christian should be."

At the 1996 commencement Dr. Sahly presented Jack with the Distinguished Service Medallion, an award voted by Southern's faculty, Jack's colleagues. Students and audience immediately rose to a standing ovation.

Former students are quick to acknowledge the effect their beloved teacher has had on their lives. "Elder Blanco infected us with the love of Jesus. He taught with such excitement and energy, you just *had* to get to know Christ better," said Cindy Frost, now a nurse in Chattanooga.

Evan Valencia, a pastor in the Gulf States Conference, remembers coming to Southern's campus a little uncertain of what he had gotten his wife and daughters into. That first Sabbath afternoon a knock sounded at their door. It was Dr. and Mrs. Blanco dropping by for a chat to get better acquainted and to pray with them. "The Holy Spirit must have led them to know we needed encouragement. Any time I needed advice or counsel, Dr. Blanco always stopped what he was doing and took time to help me," Pastor Evan said. "I feel that I have seen Christ reflected in his life."

Jack and Marion have come to realize the reward in knowing that their busy lives have not only been dedicated to God, but have also been joyous and satisfying.

When asked if he had any regrets about his life—anything he would do differently if he could—without hesitation he answered, "I could never give less than 100 percent to my Lord who saved me, but I wish I could have spent more time with my children when they were young. I love them so much. But my Father has been good, and His providence has proved abundant and merciful in every way."

Jack strongly believes that Jesus is coming soon. "A lot of the world still needs to hear of God's amazing grace and love," he says, "but just look at the ways that that can be accomplished now. These are *exciting* times!" His heart goes out to believers everywhere, but especially to those in China and Russia who risk so much when they accept Christ. Visiting those places and seeing their faith makes him want to do much more.

And what if he must, before Jesus comes, have to lay aside the challenges and decisions that come with being dean of the School of Religion at a growing university? "My Father will continue to advance His kingdom," he smiles confidently.